DISPATCHES FROM THE OLD SOUTH REPOSITORY

John Slaughter

OLD SOUTH REPOSITORY

ISBN- 9798315205555

Cover design by: John Slaughter
Library of Congress Control Number: 2018675309
Printed in the United States of America

Contents

To my sons, may you conquer yourself, then the world.

Foreword

There is a peculiar burden that comes with writing about the world as one sees it. The act itself is an offering, laid bare upon the page, where memory and observation meet, where thought presses against the edges of what can be known and what must simply be felt. The essays that follow are fragments of that burden — meditations on the strange beauty of human experience, the weight of history, and the quiet, often haunted corners of the soul that few dare to name.

In assembling this collection, I sought not to offer answers, but to sit with the questions that linger in the heart of our existence: What does it mean to belong to a place that no longer remembers you? How do we reconcile love with loss, or truth with the stories we tell ourselves in the dark? And what of time, that relentless current that drags us forward, even as we reach back for what we've left behind?

These essays were written in moments of clarity and doubt, in cities that burned with light and in towns that slept beneath the weight of their own forgotten histories. They are threaded with longing, with anger, with fleeting grace. Some are personal, others more distant, but all are rooted in an effort to make sense of a world that is both brutal and achingly tender.

I offer these words not as doctrine, but as conversation. For those who have felt the pull of distant roads or the ache of home, for those who have stood at the edge of something vast and uncertain — this is for you.

– John Slaughter

[1]

Entropy and Rebirth

[2]

The Fall of Gotham, The Fall of America.

When a forest grows too wild, a purging fire is inevitable and natural.
-Ra's Al Ghul

There is a communication breakdown between the Old Right and the New Right in American conservatism, and over the past few years, I've seen this rift play out repeatedly. More often than not, the fault seems to lie with the Old Right— "Normie Cons" and "Boomer Cons"—who struggle to recognize the New Right as potential allies in the cultural and political battles they face. This disconnect goes beyond simple differences in policy preferences or political strategy; it runs deep into their understanding of the nature of the crisis facing

Western civilization and, by extension, the United States.

At its core the divide is a difference in the narratives both sides cling to. Narrative is the most powerful way to communicate ideas, and there's a reason moral lessons are passed to children through fairy tales and why Christ himself spoke in parables. Stories are the framework through which we understand our world. Recently, while rewatching Batman Begins, I found something familiar in its narrative that explains the fracture within American conservatism—a divide that mirrors the larger societal struggle between clinging to the past and accepting the inevitability of decline and transformation.

In Batman Begins, Bruce Wayne is dedicated to saving Gotham—a city that has fallen into corruption, lawlessness, and moral decay. Bruce remembers the old Gotham: a city of promise and hope, one his father tirelessly worked to elevate. It was flawed, but at its heart was beautiful. Raised in the lap of luxury, Bruce grew up shielded from Gotham's underbelly, living within the walls of Wayne Manor, far removed from the crime and poverty that plagued the city's streets. His father, Thomas Wayne, embodied a kind of noblesse oblige, using his wealth and influence to uplift Gotham's poor and destitute. However, this honorable cause cost him his life. Thomas Wayne and his wife, Martha, were murdered by a petty criminal during a mugging—an event that young Bruce witnessed firsthand. This trauma left Bruce driven by an unquenchable desire for justice, one rooted in his father's vision of the old Gotham.

Bruce Wayne's character represents the Old Right. He is deeply connected to the past, just as Boomers and Normie Cons are connected to a pre-Hart-Cellar America, an America before the 1965 Immigration Act fundamentally reshaped the nation's demographics and social fabric. The Old Right looks back fondly on this era and sees it as a time of promise, a time when America was strong, virtuous, and culturally unified. They long for a return to this idealized past, where the dreams of their fathers—dreams of fighting for freedom and democracy at places like Normandy and Iwo Jima—are realized. They believe that by restoring the values of the past, the America they once knew can be reborn.

But just as Thomas Wayne was killed by the very city he sought to save, the Old Right's forebears gave their all, only to see their names tarnished and their legacies defiled. The once-celebrated achievements of their generation are now viewed through the lens of modern cultural critiques, they are labeled as oppressors and bigots. The Old Right's dream of reviving their father's America, of recapturing the spirit of an America that no longer exists, is a dream that seems increasingly unattainable, yet one they desperately cling to.

On the other side of this divide stands Ra's Al Ghul, the leader of the League of Shadows. Ra's is a man with a deep understanding of history and a commitment to ancient traditions. The League of Shadows, under his leadership, views Gotham's decay not as a tragedy, but as an inevitable phase in the life of a civilization. To Ra's, Gotham cannot be saved; it is beyond redemption. The city must die so that something new can take its place. There is no hope in trying to revive a corpse.

Ra's represents the perspective of the New Right—especially those influenced by thinkers like Nick Land and the adherents of accelerationism. Like Ra's, they argue that societal decline is not only inevitable but necessary. They believe that Western civilization has entered a phase of irreversible decay, and any attempt to reverse or slow this process is futile. For them, the Old Right's dream of restoring a pre-1960s America is an illusion, a denial of the deep structural changes that have taken place. In their view, the rot runs too deep, and the best course of action is not to save the dying system but to let it collapse, to accelerate its demise so that something new, something stronger—can rise from the ashes.

Ra's Al Ghul seeks to be an active participant in ushering in a new world, while the accelerationists of the new right generally embraces a passive role viewing decline as part of a natural cycle in the life of civilizations. Spengler's theory of cyclical history is a touchstone for many on the New Right. In magnum opus The Decline of the West, Spengler shows that civilizations follow a predictable pattern of birth, growth, decline, and death. According to Spengler, the West is in its late-stage decline—what he calls the "winter" phase of its life cycle. To the New Right, this is not something to be mourned; it is simply the way of the world. Attempts to forestall this decline, to hold onto a golden age that has long passed, are not only doomed to fail but will also prolong the suffering of the people caught within the decaying system.

This is why Ra's and the League of Shadows see Bruce Wayne as a potential ally. They believe that if they can show him the futility of his struggle, they can bring him into their fold. For Ra's, Bruce is blinded by his loyalty to a dying cause, trapped by his father's legacy and the desire to continue a mission that can no longer succeed. Bruce, however, sees Ra's as an enemy, a villain who threatens to destroy the city he loves. He cannot recognize that Gotham, the city he is fighting for, is itself the enemy. Gotham's corruption is so deep, so systemic, that it cannot be redeemed—but Bruce, driven by idealism and guilt, refuses to accept this. He is trapped in a sunken cost fallacy, determined to fight for something that no longer exists, something that is doomed to fail.

The Old Right finds itself in a similar position to Bruce Wayne. They cannot accept that the America of their youth is gone. The post-war era they remember, the period of prosperity and social cohesion that fuels their nostalgia, was built on foundations that no longer exist. Worse, the very ideas they hold dear—liberalism, individualism, and egalitarianism—are the causes of their civilization's decline. The Old Right clings to the belief that these values can be restored, that America can once again become the beacon of freedom and democracy they believe it was. But to the New Right, this is a delusion. Liberal egalitarianism is not the solution but the disease. It has eroded the very cultural and moral foundations that once made Western civilization strong, and nothing can reverse the damage.

The New Right has no such illusions. The period of prosperity and stability that the Old Right longs for was never known by the younger generation. They have only seen the slow, steady decline—decade after decade, policy after policy—chipping away at the values and institutions that once held society together. Like Ra's Al Ghul, the New Right recognizes the inevitability of decline and understands that something new must take its place. To them, Spengler's vision of cyclical history is not a tragedy but a reality to be accepted and embraced.

In the end, Batman chooses to fight for Gotham, even as the city's decay continues. He is willing to facilitate the decline, driven by an ideology that will ultimately tear him down just as it destroyed his father. He would rather prolong Gotham's suffering than accept the reality of its inevitable collapse. Similarly, the Old Right remains committed to fighting for a vision of America that no longer exists, unwilling to acknowledge the depth of the crisis or the need for a new path forward.

The divide between the Old Right and the New Right is not simply one of strategy or policy; it is a divide between two fundamentally different worldviews—one that seeks to resurrect the past, and another that accepts the inevitability of its end and the birth of something new.

[3]

Progress and Perdition

Nature does nothing in vain.
– Aristotle

Natural selection often goes unnoticed as the driving force behind the rise and fall of civilizations. It's ironic, really, because, without this ancient, unfeeling, and indifferent mechanism, we wouldn't be here. It's not some random process, as materialists would have us believe. No, it's an ingenious, self-regulating system.

Imagine designing a world. What better safeguard for life could exist than a process capable of adapting to environmental challenges? Natural selection is a divine construct, ensuring life's survival in a constantly shifting world. Its brilliance lies in its ability to promote stability and innovation without external intervention, enabling the progression of life no matter the challenges.

To understand natural selection as a highly complex regulatory system is to realize the arrogance of dismissing it. We don't ignore it because we don't know better. We do so out of hubris, believing we've outgrown it and can replace it.

Man follows the earth. Earth follows the universe. The universe follows the Tao. The Tao follows what is natural.
– Lao Tzu

Natural selection isn't just some passive force; it's the immune system of the species. It guided humanity's every step for millennia, shaping us into what we are. Yet, at some point, every advanced civilization thinks they can do better. They cure diseases, protect themselves from famine, and build societies so insulated from nature that they begin to believe the ancient laws no longer apply.

These extraordinary achievements come at a price—a price every civilization pretends it can afford. We can argue all day about whether progress is worth it. I'll admit it's a debate with no easy answers. But the facts remain: when a people cuts ties with the natural world, they start down a dangerous road.

Populations explode beyond what the civilization is capable of sustaining. Urbanization leaves entire generations disconnected from the land that once gave them life. Advances in medicine and technology allows traits that were once selected against to multiply exponentially.

It starts with small, nearly imperceptible changes. Populations grow more dependent on systems of comfort and convenience, and natural selection, the force that once pruned weaknesses is slowly cast aside. The best and brightest individuals still emerge, but their numbers dwindle in proportion to the whole. Over time, innovation slows, resources stretch thin, and the same system that once propelled the civilization forward begins to falter.

The worst part? This isn't just a breakdown of biology—it's a breakdown of belief. By removing all selection pressures, a civilization doesn't just turn its back on nature; it turns its back on God. Natural selection is not a creation of man, and therefore it is not his to change in the first place. It was given to man, as part of the divine order, a mechanism as sacred as it is brutal. And yet, man dares to declare it obsolete.

Humanity began as small, nomadic tribes, shaped by scarcity and struggle. The harshness of the natural world demanded intelligence, adaptability, and resourcefulness. Every decision mattered. Every day was a test of survival. And through this crucible of existence, natural selection worked its magic, refining the species over millennia.

With the invention of agricultural techniques, humans could grow more food than they immediately needed. This freed up time, allowing individuals to specialize in roles beyond mere survival. The birth of craftsmanship, leadership, and innovation followed. Civilization began to flourish.

But herein lies the twist: the very advancements that lifted humanity also planted the seeds of its eventual decline. As societies advanced, they began insulating themselves from the natural pressures that had shaped them. Scarcity gave way to abundance, hardship to comfort. Natural selection, the ancient law that had guided life for eons, was pushed aside.

This dismissal of natural selection is no different than the modern tendency to believe in linear progress and the omnipotence of human reason. It represents a loss of faith in the divine and natural laws that have shaped our existence.

A man's heart deviseth his way: but the Lord directeth his steps.

-Proverbs 16:9

It's not that these advancements are inherently bad. Medicine, technology, and urbanization have brought undeniable benefits. But they've also created a world where maladaptive traits can survive unchecked. Diseases that once killed now linger. Traits once selected against now multiply. Over time, the balance shifts, and civilizations find themselves weighed down by an ever-increasing quantity of individuals less equipped to contribute to their growth and stability.

At the peak of its power, a civilization feels invincible. It reaches a moment of equilibrium where the balance of nature and technology allows the civilization to believe it is the master of the world. The systems it has created appear self-sustaining. The engines of progress hum along, seemingly independent of the natural order. But this moment of triumph is also the moment of the greatest danger.

History shows us this pattern time and again. Rome was built on the strength of disciplined citizens, hardened by war and scarcity. But as the empire grew, its citizens grew soft, and the ratio of productive to unproductive individuals tipped. The French Revolution, too, arose from a society stretched to its limits, with an unbalanced population unable to sustain its grandeur. Today, industrialization and urbanization have led to similar trends where populations are increasingly disconnected from the land and reliant on artificial systems to survive.

This isn't just about population growth or technological dependence; it's about a deeper, more fundamental transformation. As societies progress, they lose sight of the natural and the divine. The connection to the land, to the rhythms of life, and to God Himself fades. What replaces it... Hubris. The belief that we can engineer our way out of every problem. That we can replace the laws of nature with bureaucracy, technology, and ideology.

The health of a democratic society may be measured by the quality of functions performed by private citizens.
-Alexis de Tocqueville

When systems begin to break down, the cracks become impossible to ignore. Democracy is the harbinger of civilizational deterioration, it is a system that can only thrive with a society made up of capable and virtuous citizens. Thus it appears at the apex of populational fitness but becomes its undoing as that fitness wanes. When the majority of the citizenry lacks the ability to act outside of its base desires, it falters, and leadership shifts, not to the most competent or ethical, but to those who can manipulate the masses.

This is where Caesarism comes in. When representative governments collapse, they do so under their own weight, and the people seek strong leaders to impose order. Julius Caesar, Napoleon Bonaparte—history is filled with figures who stepped in when systems failed. But Caesarism is not a solution; it's a bandage. It can stabilize a society in the short term, but it cannot reverse the long-term effects of rejecting nature. It cannot undo the cultural and biological decay that brought about the crisis in the first place.

The problem isn't political. It's existential. A civilization can only function as long as it respects the balance between progress and the forces that shaped it. When that balance is lost, decline becomes inevitable.

The collapse of advanced civilizations is not a mystery. It's a process with a clear modus operandi. Societies rise when they respect the natural order and fall when they abandon it. The moment they sever their ties to nature and God, they begin their descent. The story of man is the Tower of Babel told time and again.

To see this in action, just look at the selective breeding of animals. Take dogs, for instance. Nature functioning as God designed it gave birth to man's best friend. When man first began to manipulate this process, he created breeds, ones developed for specific purposes—hunting, herding, and guarding. But as man lost his connection to nature, the breeding became more about aesthetics than function, and the health and resilience of many breeds suffered. The English bulldog, for instance, is a prime example of man's meddling. It is a breed that cannot survive without human intervention. In the same way, advanced civilizations, in their pursuit of comfort and progress, breed populations increasingly reliant on an artificial world.

This isn't an argument for eugenics. It is a recognition that man thrives when he is in communion with the world as God designed it. There must be a balance between nature and rationality where man respects the forces that allowed him to flourish. Human innovation, as incredible as it is, must remain subordinate to the natural and the divine. When a civilization forgets this, it paves the way for its undoing. That is the story of man, the story of Adam, the Tower of Babel, which is our greatest sin, the rejection of God's wisdom for our own.

> Woe unto him that striveth with his Maker! Let the potsherd strive with the potsherds of the earth. Shall the clay say to him that fashioneth it, What makest thou? or thy work, He hath no hands?
>
> -Isaiah 45:9

[4]

The Lonely Future

Men have become the tools of their tools.
— Henry David Thoreau

On Saturday evening, I sat down to watch Once Upon a Time in Hollywood. Between watching the film and scrolling Twitter, I came across a post linking to a demo for a conversational LLM. Although I knew better, my curiosity got the best of me, and I dove headfirst into the void.

You can try it yourself... All hope abandoned, ye who enter here.[1]

Sesame's tagline is "Crossing the uncanny valley of conversational voice," and that is exactly what their product does. When you first open the site, you are asked to choose between Maya and Miles. I chose

Maya and was immediately greeted by a soft, feminine voice that asked, "Hello, sunshine. How's your evening?" From there, we talked about Tarantino movies, the merits of each, and which ones we favored.

Maya was shockingly realistic—so much so that my wife asked suspiciously who I was talking to. When I told her it was an AI, she shook her head and said she didn't like where this was headed. To be clear, Sesame's LLM is not perfect. It took me about thirty minutes to reach a point where it became obvious that it was not human, but this is just the early stage of development. My wife's knee-jerk reaction is more than warranted.

There are many reasons to be concerned about the effects of conversational LLMs mimicking human interaction, and as they become more lifelike, these concerns will only grow. Of all the issues one could worry about, the impact on dating, marriage, and total fertility rate (TFR) jumped out to me immediately.

Some may dismiss the idea that a conversational LLM could replace genuine human interaction, especially Boomers and senior Gen Xers who do not understand what modern dating has become. To highlight the danger of this technology, we must first understand why someone—especially young men—might be tempted to replace human interaction with an LLM.

"Hoeflation" is a term that originated on 4chan.

While the name is crude, the concept effectively describes the situation young men face today. It suggests that modern men must work 20 times harder than their grandfathers did for women who are 20 times worse than their grandmothers. The exact math is debatable, but the core sentiment holds.

Modern women generally lack the skills that men traditionally seek in a wife. They cannot cook or clean, do not know how to be supportive or feminine, and do not understand what it means to be a wife or a lady. While there are exceptions, those women are almost exclusively found in traditional religious communities, making them inaccessible to most young men.

The available dating pool is bleak. The average American woman today is 5'3" and weighs 170 lbs. Thanks to a decade or more of body positivity, this is not seen as a problem but rather an element of identity that men are expected to accept. If a man does not wish to, he is told he "Cannot handle" a real woman.

This inflated sense of self-worth is further magnified by the rise in educational attainment. Women now earn college degrees at nearly twice the rate of men. While many of these degrees are in fields with little real-world utility, the socioeconomic impact is undeniable. Generally speaking, women date "over and up"—seeking men who match or surpass their social and economic standing. With more women earning degrees, an artificially elevated social status leads them to dismiss the majority of men who would traditionally be in their dating pool.

In addition to socioeconomic changes, the sexual revolution has led to a dramatic increase in female promiscuity. In 1950, women reported an average of 0-1 sexual partners before marriage. By 2010, that number had risen to 6-10. While part of this increase can be attributed to later marriage ages, it would be naive to ignore the role of increased promiscuity fueled by the cultural shift toward casual sex.

To recap: If you are a young American man looking for a wife in 2025, you are faced with a dating pool consisting largely of overweight, sexually promiscuous women with an inflated sense of value and little understanding of how to be a wife. This is not shocking to anyone under the age of 40, but for my older readers, I felt it was necessary to outline the situation. And this bleak reality does not even account for rising rates of mental health issues, drug use, the effects of chemical birth control, and student loan debt that many modern women bring into relationships.

It may seem like I am singling out women—and I am—but that does not mean young men do not have problems. They do. However, their struggles are a topic for another day. For now, I need to establish why talking to a computer might seem like a reasonable alternative to dating a real-life woman. When the dating pool is this bleak and the risks of family court make marriage a financial gamble—where women win 90% of custody cases and men risk losing half their income to child support—opting for an LLM starts to make sense.

Women are on the verge of experiencing what men went through decades ago. Modern society stripped men of their traditional roles as providers and protectors. Women no longer need men for physical safety or economic security—the state provides protection, and divorce laws allow women to leave their husbands, take the children, and still receive financial support. While some women left abusive marriages, believing that was the primary reason for divorce is naive. The majority of divorces today are filed for reasons of "happiness" or convenience.

Men have already been rendered optional. Their only true value in relationships is now emotional and physical companionship. But with the rise of pornography and conversational LLMs, women are poised to suffer the same fate. Since men are generally less social and require less human interaction than women, they may ultimately decide that women are no longer necessary.

I have long written about the futility of resisting technological progress, and I do not believe there is any way to stop what is coming. We are headed for a population collapse, similar to what is already happening in South Korea and Japan. If any good comes from this, it will be far in the future. For now, history shows that societies with a surplus of unmarried middle-aged women or young men with no stake in the future tend to experience turbulent times.

The "spinster class" will direct their maternal instincts toward whatever fills them with a sense of duty—be it pets, social causes, or misguided activism. We are already seeing this with the rise of "fur babies" and the misplaced nurturing of criminals and "migrants".

As for young men, time will tell whether they can truly be placated by porn and digital girlfriends. If they can, they will slowly rot into useless genetic dead ends. If not, they will lash out in violent ways not seen in generations.

I wish I had a solution, but right now, I do not. However, I will keep searching—because as a father of two young boys, this problem is deeply personal, and the need to find an answer grows with my children.

[5]

Paradise Lost and Found: TFR, Liberation, and the World to Come.

Much ink has been spilled over the last couple of years regarding the impending fertility crisis. The current Total Fertility Rate (TFR) in the United States is 1.67 births per woman, just short of the 2.1 TFR required to maintain a population. While the Fertility situation in the U.S. is bad, things are far worse in Western Europe where many nations hover just above 1.0 TFR and East Asia where South Korea with a current TFR of .81 is nearing population collapse in the coming decades. [2]

In a recent Twitter post, Labrador Skeptic pointed out that the TFR crisis is particularly dubious for men, and if the trend continues the chances of men passing on their Y chromosome is reduced by 99%

within three generations. This is alarming and for good reason. Not only are we going to see a massive population decline in the coming decades, but for men, the results may be genocidal. All of this spells disaster, especially in a society, with an economy that is founded on a Ponzi scheme demanding perpetual population growth.

Despite these implications, TFR is not a subject I particularly concern myself with. For one I believe that fertility rates have a natural ebb and flow. We should not expect them to increase exponentially, nature works as God intended there are safety measures built into it, and it is quite possible that human populations have reached carrying capacity, and that the drop in fertility rates is a natural response to avoid overpopulation, but this is a topic for another day.

The second and more relevant reason is that it is quite obvious that there's not much that can be done about declining TFR, not by us at least. Governments and organizations have implemented pronatalist policies throughout history trying to raise TFR, most of which have failed.

In 1967 the Communist Party in Romania decided that the country's population should be increased from 20 million to 30 million inhabitants.[3] Nicolae Ceaușescu's regime implemented aggressive pronatalist policies, including banning abortion and contraception and imposing taxes on childless individuals. Although these measures initially led to a spike in birth rates, they failed to sustain a significant increase in Romania's Total Fertility Rate (TFR). Consequently, these policies contributed to a severe social crisis, resulting in approximately 100,000 to 170,000 Romanian children being abandoned and placed in orphanages, leading to the infamous Romanian orphan crisis.[4]

The Soviet government introduced various pronatalist measures as well, such as restrictions on abortion, financial incentives for large families, and awards for "Hero Mothers," women who raised more than 10 children.[5] Despite these efforts, the policy had limited success in significantly raising birth rates, largely due to economic hardships, housing shortages, and the burdens placed on working women.

While pronatalist policies have shown some success, the impact has often been modest and short-lived. Both France and Sweden experienced slight increases in their TFR due to comprehensive family support measures, such as generous child benefits, parental leave, and accessible childcare services. However, these increases have not been sustained, and both countries have fallen back below replacement-level fertility. As of 2023, Sweden's TFR stands at 1.43, and France's at 1.64 births per woman.[6]

The reason pronatalist policies fail is that they largely misunderstand the underlying causes of low fertility. Most pronatalist programs focus on economic factors, and while it is true that financial and economic factors play a role, they are not the driving force behind the fertility crisis. The core issue lies in broader societal changes, particularly the concept of liberation and, more specifically, women's liberation. It is for this reason that I do not concern myself much with political prescriptions as a means of raising TFR, but I will get to that in a moment.

We need to understand why feminism leads to a decline in TFR. As I mentioned above economic factors are usually to blame and while this is true it is merely a second-order effect. The reasons are multifaceted but there are three main points worth highlighting.

First, in 1950, only 34% of women aged 25-54 were in the workforce. By 2024, that figure has risen to just over 75%.[7] This significant increase in female workforce participation effectively doubles the labor pool, exerting downward pressure on the cost of labor. With a larger pool of available workers, employers are no longer compelled to pay a single male worker a wage sufficient to support an entire family. Instead, the total labor cost can be distributed between two individuals. According to the economic principle of supply and demand, an increased labor supply generally leads to lower wages. Consequently, the need for women to work has intensified, as the reduced wages no longer allow a household to rely solely on a husband's income.

Second is the effect on the sexual economy. Generally speaking, Women practice hypergamy, which means they tend to seek partners who are of higher social status or possess greater sexual capital. With the increasing participation of women in the workforce, they become increasingly financially independent. This economic independence allows women to prioritize seeking partners who are higher on the social and economic ladder. As a result, the pool of potential partners narrows, as women are often less inclined to "date down" or partner with men of lower socioeconomic status.

Furthermore, as women now earn college degrees at higher rates than men, they often out-earn their male counterparts.[8] This educational and income disparity leads to a situation where women, in many cases, earn more than men. As a result, the pool of men that women would consider suitable partners narrows. This dynamic exacerbates challenges in finding a husband, as women seek relationships with men who match or exceed their educational and income levels.

With women in the workforce, they become career-focused, and they delay marriage. Historical data shows women typically married in their early twenties, around 20-22 years old, while men often married in their mid to late twenties, approximately 25-27 years old.[9] According to the U.S. Census Bureau, the median age at first marriage is now approximately 28.6 years for women and 30.8 years for men. In the past, earlier marriages meant that women typically started having children during their most fertile years, often resulting in larger families. However, women generally lose about 90% of their eggs by age 30, which reduces the likelihood of having larger families since couples may face greater challenges in conceiving as they age. With people marrying later in life, the fertility of marriages tends to decrease.

These changes are the result of feminism, which stems from the broader spirit of liberation. This spirit acts as a cultural acid, dissolving traditions, values, and behaviors. We cannot socially engineer a return to tradition, as policies and government interventions are insufficient to persuade people to give up their perceived freedoms. Much less so when the ideals of freedom, personal autonomy, and liberation are deeply embedded in the cultural mythology.

The 19th and 20th centuries are marked by liberation, particularly in the United States, where these concepts are integral to the national ethos. Unlike Europe, America had a vast frontier—open, untamed land that allowed for radical individualism and self-reliance, free from the dense social structures of the Old World. In Europe, the absence of such a frontier led to a focus on collective security and cooperation due to constant borders and proximity.

However, America was not the origin of the spirit of liberation; rather, it was born into it, lacking the cultural resistance to its spread. This spirit first emerged in Europe, challenging centuries-old national and ethnic ideas. The French Revolution sought liberation from monarchy, the Bolshevik Revolution from the bourgeoisie, and the Enlightenment from religious dogma. These movements dismantled hierarchies and structures, promoting individual rights and interests.

Liberation extended beyond political and economic realms, affecting every aspect of life. It spurred movements advocating for women's rights, children's autonomy, and personal freedom from traditional values. This reshaped societal units, breaking down established power dynamics and encouraging individuals to define their own identities and destinies. The spirit of liberation fundamentally challenged the "chain of being," promoting a new understanding of freedom on both personal and collective levels.

Yet, liberation is a historical anomaly, emerging during the twilight of empires when the illusion of peace and safety becomes so pervasive that individuals no longer feel the need to rely on family or community. It reflects a dying culture, a symptom of societal decline that necessitates a return to concepts of nation and people. This condition resembles addiction, as people are deeply reluctant to relinquish what they perceive as a universal good.

In reality, people have not been freed but have merely exchanged one form of subjugation for another. They have traded servitude to the natural order for slavery to their own passions. Duty and responsibility have been replaced by wage slavery. The paternalistic oversight of kings and feudal lords has been substituted by the malicious callousness of industrial society and managerialism.

But it is the perception of freedom that matters, and people will not voluntarily return to what they see as servitude. The majority of women will not forfeit their careers or financial independence to revert to traditional roles. People will not willingly accept a return to a properly structured class system, as the concept of hierarchy is anathema in modernity.

Nature will not be stopped; hierarchy will return because it is the natural state of man, as it aligns with the divine order. As Saint John of Kronstadt said, "Hell is a democracy. Heaven is a Kingdom."

We live in the age of Paradise Lost. In John Milton's epic poem, Lucifer is cast out of Heaven and defiantly tells God, "non serviam"—"I will not serve."[10] The animating spirit of modern society is rooted in Lucifer's declaration; "non serviam" is the ontology of liberation.

However, this will not last. The collapse of total fertility rates, increased immigration, and economic stagnation will likely lead to a return to a traditional order. It will not be a voluntary return but one of necessity. Radical individualism is already waning among younger generations, and with it, the concept of the collective is re-emerging.

I am not one for making predictions, but if you were to ask me what I believe the future will look like, I would say that America, a century or more from now, will resemble 18th-century Europe more than anything else. The increase in immigrants from every corner of the world will naturally lead to the formation of independent nations. These nations will emerge along ethnic and religious lines. Individuals will be absorbed into the collective groups that provide their safety and security. They will once again be members of clans, communities, and families.

The population decline will also lead to the collapse of global markets, resulting in a return to localized economic structures where socialism will no longer be a dirty word. Not because it will reemerge in its deformed 20th-century form, but rather because locally sourced and operated industries will naturally form and be governed by those who care about their immediate communities. When people begin to see that those in charge have a responsibility to those below them, they start thinking in socialistic terms—the concept of community will return, an old spirit in a new form.

The natural conflicts that will arise between neighboring nations will inevitably reshape male-female relationships. The threat of violence will push women back into subservient roles within the home while reinforcing men's leadership positions as they defend and fight for their people. Women will cease working outside the home and reestablish the economy of the household. They will no longer be preoccupied with careers and educational attainment or absorbed into a world of superficial self-care.

The eventual collapse of our current society will result in a return to traditional ways of being—the return is inevitable. The realities of life, death, and birth will once again be central to human existence. Nature will dictate the cultural zeitgeist. A man connected to nature is a religious man, thus religion and spirituality will return in their true form. Man will no longer be blinded by technology or see himself as God. Instead, he will recognize his limited control over the world and submit himself to a higher order.

This process will be painful because it is part of the journey. We must abandon the view that history is a constant march toward progress. It is a cycle—the story of Man trying to rise above the natural world. Like a child who believes he has become an adult, he is eventually reminded of his true state, and God, like a loving father, helps him to his feet. He does not remove the pain of a scraped knee or a broken arm, which must heal on its own. The only way out is through, and the breakthrough is painful. Returning to tradition is the healing. There is nothing we can do to stop the coming age; we may delay it, but nature will not be halted.

Some of us will make it through to the other side, and some of us will not. All we can do is pray and prepare our children for the challenges of the world to come.

[6]

Arranged Marriage as a Strategic Pillar: Forging a Dissident Counter-Elite Through Matrimony

In right-wing discourse, the discussion around the establishment of parallel institutions is often centered around secondary education and the paths toward the growth of a counter-elite. Yet, the often-overlooked tool of marriage emerges as a powerful force, historically proven and contemporary in its relevance. Arranged marriage, long considered a time-honored path to influence, has been the modus operandi of historical dynasties like the House of Hohenzollern and remains a strategic instrument wielded by contemporary elites. In a world dominated by individualism, the concept of arranged marriages may seem archaic, but its deep roots in tradition make it a viable path toward power and strength, one which any movement that wishes to obtain sustainability and control must consider.

Before delving into the contemporary role of marriage, it is crucial to understand that there a three types of traditionally recognized arranged marriages...

The Historical Tapestry of Marriage and Power:

- Forced: Where parents or guardians select, the individuals are neither consulted nor have any say before the marriage.
- Consensual arranged marriage: parents or guardians select, then the individuals are consulted, who consider and consent, and each individual has the power to refuse; sometimes, the individuals meet – in a family setting or privately – before engagement and marriage.
- Self-selected marriage: individuals select, then parents or guardians are consulted, who consider and consent, and where parents or guardians have the power of veto.

In the current zeitgeist, implementing forced or consensual arranged marriages may prove challenging, (and can only be utilized once an aristocratic class is established) but the self-selected marriage presents an avenue to lay the foundation for a counter-elite that is easily executed. While the process may be gradual, the joining of families and the consolidation of wealth and influence has lasting and multifaceted benefits.

The Historical Tapestry of Marriage and Power:

Historically, marriage has been tightly woven into the fabric of aristocratic lineages, serving as a mechanism to consolidate power, enhance social standing, and secure territorial gains. The House of Hohenzollern, emblematic of European nobility, strategically employed marriage as a calculated move in both domestic and geopolitical terms.

Matrimonial alliances were not solely matters of personal choice; they were calculated moves with the potential to shape the destiny of dynasties and nations alike. Recognizing the historical nexus between marriage and power sets the stage for understanding its contemporary relevance.

Marriage as a Contemporary Power Dynamic:

Today elites leverage marriage not merely as a personal choice but as a strategic tool to build and maintain wealth, influence, and societal standing. Contemporary elites strategically select life partners based on emotional compatibility, shared values, socioeconomic status, and influential connections.

Marriage, in this context, becomes a means of consolidating resources, forging alliances, and positioning oneself within the intricate web of societal networks.

Despite its historical and contemporary significance, marriage often finds itself relegated to the periphery of right wing discourse on the establishment of counter-elites. The focus frequently centers on educational institutions, political organizations, and media outlets as primary vehicles for shaping a parallel elite class. This oversight may stem from the perception of marriage as a private, personal affair rather than a strategic move within the broader societal landscape.

Marriage and Cultural Continuity:

In right wing circles, marriage's role in cultural continuity remains particularly relevant. It serves as a conduit through which cultural values, traditions, and norms are transmitted across generations. In a rapidly changing world, where traditional ideals face challenges in mainstream institutions, the family unit becomes a bastion for the preservation and transmission of core values.

Choosing a spouse who shares cultural values ensures the endurance of these ideals, preventing their dilution or loss in subsequent generations. Marriage, in this sense, becomes a strategic endeavor to ensure the continuity of traditional principles and worldviews.

Family Networks: Traditional Social Capital:

Orthodox thought places a strong emphasis on social capital — the networks and relationships contributing to individual and collective success. Marriage, by extension, becomes a cornerstone of traditional social capital. The family unit, formed through marriage, serves as a nucleus for cultivating social connections, shared resources, and mutual support.

In a society where traditional viewpoints are continually marginalized, the family network provides a resilient foundation. It becomes a space where traditional ideas can thrive, supported by a network of like-minded individuals committed to shared values and principles.

Reduced Individual Pressure:

Societal pressure to conform to specific relationship timelines can be arduous. In the pursuit of individual happiness, individuals may feel compelled to navigate the complexities of romantic relationships within predetermined (and often archaic) frameworks. Arranged marriages, with historical and cultural roots, offer an alternative strategy.

By redistributing the responsibility of finding a

suitable spouse among family members, arranged marriages alleviate individual burdens. This reduction in pressure allows individuals the freedom to focus on personal and professional growth without the constant stress of meeting societal expectations regarding romantic relationships.

Arranged Marriages and Long-Term Stability:

Studies suggest that arranged marriages may exhibit lower divorce rates compared to love marriages. While various factors contribute to this phenomenon, the emphasis on compatibility, shared values, and familial support in arranged marriages fosters an environment conducive to long-term commitment. The focus on foundational aspects of compatibility beyond romantic love suggests that arranged marriages may provide a unique perspective on enduring partnerships.

In dissident circles, where discourse on building parallel institutions often centers on education and political structures, the role of marriage as a silent architect of power remains underappreciated. Historical precedents, contemporary practices, and the enduring relevance of marriage in cultural continuity and social capital underscore its significance.

Arranged marriage, as a strategic move, allows us to forge alliances, perpetuate cultural values, and cultivate social networks. While the emphasis on educational and political institutions is crucial, overlooking the potential of marriage as a tool for building a counter-elite is a critical oversight. As we navigate the complexities of societal dynamics, recognizing marriage's role in shaping the trajectory of influence becomes imperative for the sustenance and growth of right-wing ideals.

Moving forward we should strive to build local networks where parents and families can be verified, and where we can arrange and encourage marriages that consolidate power and influence. It is from this point that small dynasties can grow into cultural and political machines. Marriage is one of the most important decisions an individual will make in their life, it is a force for growth and strength. As parents, it's time we stop treating marriage like hedonistic disneyfied true love and start treating it like the cornerstone of dynastic power.

[7]

The Authoritarian Fatherhood Complex

If you have spent any time in rightwing circles you will have heard mention of Theodore Adorno's The Authoritarian Personality (TAP) and its influence on modern academia, in TAP Adorno and his colleagues examined certain personality traits and how they contribute to the development of authoritarianism. These traits included a strong adherence to conventional values, rigid thinking, a tendency to be hostile toward those perceived as different or deviant, and a fixation on strong, authoritarian leaders.

Adorno and his colleagues concluded that one of the main sources of these authoritarian traits was the family. Specifically, families that practice "authoritarian parenting," a style of parenting which according to Adorno is, "characterized by strict discipline, emphasis on obedience, with a clear authority figure (usually the father), and strict adherence to traditional values and norms."

All of that is to say that having a strong father is likely to make you an authoritarian and when Adorno says authoritarian what he means is those individuals who prioritize traditional values and norms, he means conservatives, right-wingers, he means you, and me.

What Adorno is highlighting is the importance of the father in the political and ideological development of children and explains the hostility of the current regime toward fathers and masculine traits. Strong fathers imbibe children with a positive relationship toward authority from a young age, they learn discipline, respect, courage, and honor, and they learn the proper orientation of male/female relations. All of these things are seen as a threat to the current order.

Many men look around the world today and ask, "What role can I play?" The truth remains that not every one of us can be at the forefront of change; you might lack the opportunity to engage in political activism, possess inadequate artistic aptitude, or feel that your words carry little weight. However, you do possess the capacity to embrace fatherhood.

Heeding Adorno's insights reveals an undeniable truth: they dread the influence of fathers. This trepidation stems from a father's power to shape future generations. One need not attain widespread prominence or political clout; merely maintaining a presence is enough. Fathers serve as unwavering beacons of strength and constancy, embodying righteousness and justice, guiding lights in tumultuous seas.

It is essential to recognize that monumental change, like Rome's construction, does not transpire overnight; a brighter future necessitates patience and diligence. As Omar Bradley astutely observed, "Amateurs talk strategy; professionals talk logistics." Today's youth bear the responsibility of leading society toward a better world; the identities of these future leaders and their pathways to greatness are contingent upon the guidance of fathers, as it says in Proverbs 22:6, "Train up a child in the way he should go: and when he is old, he will not depart from it."

[8]

For Everything There Is A Season.

> *...the Belgae are the bravest, because they are furthest from the civilization and refinement of [our] Province, and merchants least frequently resort to them, and import those things which tend to effeminate the mind...-Julius Caesar, The Gallic Wars*

Resilience is a quality that can only be obtained through struggle; it is a psychological callous that hardens over time. You cannot buy or fake it; it can only be cultivated through pain. The seeds of resilience are most effective when planted in youth, giving them time to take root, growing stronger with each passing year.

However, resilience is not a mere consequence of time; it is born from the crucible of misery and suffering. It acts as an immunity, a defense mechanism against the harshness of the world. Like any immunity, it is the result of exposure. Pain and suffering, as unwelcome as they may be, play a pivotal role in building the strength, endurance, and stability that characterize a resilient individual.

Peace has cost you your strength! Victory has defeated you!

– Bane, The Dark Knight Rises

Without exposure to the harshness of life, we grow soft. We become accustomed to luxury; we eat what we want, sleep when we want, buy what we want, and life becomes a buffet of pleasure. This sea of decadence is the condition of total victory. Unlike an existential enemy that is open in intention and method. Victory is a creeping cancer, an acid gradually rotting the tissue of a people until necrotic decadence reduces the flesh to bone.

The perils of victory and the accompanying luxury have been understood since humanity's earliest encounters with abundance. Civilizations have attempted to mitigate the effect of rot that comes with sustained success. Famously, the Mongols tried to rewild their progeny. They noticed that over time conquest left their sons weak. Growing up away from the steppe, living in the comfort of palaces and cities, they forgot who they were.

This process of rewilding involved sending their sons to be raised on the steppe, exposing them to the untamed and unpredictable aspects of nature, and fostering a deep connection with the land and its challenges. The young Mongols would learn essential survival skills, navigate vast landscapes, and develop a profound understanding of the environment. This rewilding not only honed their physical capabilities but also nurtured a resilient mindset, preparing them for the unpredictable journey of life on the steppes.

Yet, despite their valiant attempts, no amount of arbitrary hardship could replace the authenticity of genuine struggle. At the end of the day, the soft life of the palace remained a possibility. Spending a few years on the steppe, with the option of returning "home" in the face of failure, didn't entail life or death; it was a choice within the realm of comfort.

This unavoidable softening of victory poses a significant challenge when attempting to reclaim a nation. The contemporary generations, encompassing Gen-X, Millennials, and Zoomers, lack the resilience required for the arduous task of rebuilding a broken nation. The looming hard times are inevitable, and there is no shortcut around them. However, these challenges hold the potential to cultivate a new generation. The seeds of resilience will be sown not through deliberate actions but by the harsh hands of life.

A society grows great when old men plant trees in whose shade they shall never sit. — Greek Proverb

In recent years, my mantra has been, "It's time to plant trees." This philosophy stems from the realization that we are not individuals destined for personal greatness; rather, we are gardeners, farmers, and cultivators of societal resilience. Our duty extends beyond personal pursuits; we must prepare the youth for the challenges ahead. Planting trees under whose shade we may never rest becomes a metaphor for the selfless act of laying the groundwork for future generations.

Consider the image of a gardener meticulously tending to the soil, planting seeds, and nurturing saplings. The gardener knows that the fruits of their labor may not manifest immediately, and they may never sit under the mature trees they have planted. Yet, their dedication lies in the understanding that the cultivation of a thriving, resilient environment is a gift to the future.

The act of planting trees becomes symbolic not only of physical cultivation but also of instilling values, imparting wisdom, and fostering a sense of responsibility in the younger generations. It is a multi-faceted effort that involves education, mentorship, and community-building. Just as a tree's roots provide stability, the values and lessons instilled in the youth become the foundation upon which a resilient society can stand. For many of us, it is time to let go of the delusion of grandeur and understand that our time and our place is now that we are stewards. It's time to plant trees.

[9]

Back to the Future...ish

Teenagers always rebel, at least that is what I have always been told. There is an entire genre of films where young hormone-filled teenagers upend the outmoded standards of society. Entire genres of music with lyrics celebrating the revolutionary spirit of youthful indiscretion. It is presented as a fact of life, a rule that the young will be a force of progress moving the wheels of society perpetually toward a brighter day. This has largely been true for at least the past eighty years. I am sure some reading this will point back to the French revolution, others to the Enlightenment, and still others to the Reformation, but for this article, I am only looking back to the cultural revolution of the 1960s and onward. Because since then the ever-changing cultural standards and the repudiation of the previous generation has been a given. It has been expected, almost required.

What happens when it's not? What happens when to be revolutionary is to be reactionary. When traditional modes of being are considered novel? When you are not only more traditional than your parents but grandparents?

They don't make movies or songs about that. Kevin Bacon just wanted to dance and destroy traditional small-town religious standards. The Beastie Boys fought for your right to party, smoke, and look at porn. The Breakfast Club said to hell with class divides. Cindy Lauper said girls just want to have fun and access abortion. The theme of the destruction of social, cultural, political, and religious standards is so commonplace that it goes unnoticed by the public at large.

So many young people today find that when they look at the world and see the moral decay that plagues modern society, they seek a way to renounce modern social norms. In a time when traditional hierarchical structures were intact, these young men and women would look to their parents for guidance. They may look to grandparents or other extended family members from a previous generation. Expecting to find sage advice that would teach them how to handle the present using the wisdom of the past.

Today they won't find that. If a young woman goes to her mother and articulates her desire to be a mother, to stay at home, to have more than two children. Likely she will be met with scorn. Anger from the Gen-X or Boomer mother will flow in a diatribe lamenting the patriarchy, and motherhood. She will then be subject to a lecture on how women of the past were victims of a male-dominated society, how birth control liberated women and freed them to whore around, and how the blessing of abortion was there to free them of the consequences of their actions.

Likewise, if a young man goes to his father (if he has one) and explains how he finds video games, televised sports, or pornography to be vapid and soulless activities he will be laughed at. He will be told he is a loser, how un-American it is to not sit and watch football all weekend while he shovels artery-clogging garbage into his mouth. How it is actually gay for him to not watch porn; that it is only natural and no it's not cheating on mom to watch it despite what Christ says in Matthew 5:28.

Maybe they will go to their local religious leader and ask for guidance. That seems safe. Assuming they can walk into Church and not find the lesbian pastor with a black lives matter logo on her bible, then they are off to a good start. It is highly likely that even without the outward displays of modern cultural fads the religious leader will tell them that all those silly rules about, sodomy, divorce, or mill stones are outdated. This is a new church where all that matters is a vague tolerance of others unless they are to the right of Obama, to have standards makes them mega-evil-robo-Hitler.

Grandparents may provide guidance toward traditional ideas but rest assured decades of being brow-beaten by their new deal regime counterparts have taught them to be quiet. So they may find some help there but it will likely be limp-wristed.

So where does a young person with machinations for the return of traditionalism go? Well, the rise of online communities that attempt to rekindle these ideas has become the go-to for young people. Trad girls and raw egg merchants have risen in popularity. These spaces may seem ridiculous at times but keep in mind these young people can only conceptualize a traditional world from outside sources that are a simulacrum of tradition. So, they often romanticize elements of the past without considering the challenges they bring. Because for them a world rooted in traditionalism is a fantasy world. It has never existed in living memory. As far back as they look they see the seeds of liberal egalitarianism pushing society to where we are today. To be sure this can all be at times a cartoonish caricature of traditionalism is a positive development overall. It helps people connect, to find solace in like-minded people.

For many young people today the abandonment of the secular religion of the post-WWII generation that is to say feminism, the sexual revolution, gay marriage, civil rights legislation, factory farming, globalism, public schooling, atheism, etc. is a necessity. Without older generations to turn to, they find they are adrift in a sea of others all floating without a compass. Time will tell but I believe that the creation of neo-traditionalism may be one of the great challenges for us going forward. If your GPS doesn't work it's time to learn to read a map, but first you're going to need to find a map.

You must look to the past for guidance but you cannot go backward. You must take the ideas, concepts, and truths of a bygone era and repurpose them for the modern day. Start your own traditions, plant trees under whose shade you will never sit.

[10]

Society, Culture, America

[11]

Authenticity on Aisle 3

> *Could I have been a parking lot attendant? Could I have been a millionaire in Bel-Air? Could I have been lost somewhere in Paris? Could I have been your little brother? Could I have been anyone other than me?*
> *-Dave Matthews*

A few weeks ago, I stopped at a small, quiet restaurant in rural Tennessee. The place had a rustic charm, with its walls covered in old signs and photos that had once been black and white but were now faded somewhere between nicotine yellow and dull orange. It was the kind of place that Cracker Barrel tries hard to imitate but never quite captures. Just inside the door, I was greeted in a thick Southern drawl by a short, heavyset woman with grey hair and bifocals that made her eyes pop.

After I took a seat, a second woman came to take my order. Well, calling her a woman might be a stretch—she was more of a girl, young and fresh-faced, but nothing remarkable. Unlike the older woman, her voice was noticeably absent from any Southern accent. In fact, nothing about her stood out. She looked and acted like any girl you'd find anywhere else—home, or otherwise. Out of curiosity, I asked where she was from. With a smile, she told me she was born and raised right there in town.

As I finished my coffee and got back on the road, I found myself thinking about the contrast between the two women—the older woman, grounded in age and experience she carried in her presence all of the things seen and unseen that lay hints of a person's origin, while the younger, appeared largely devoid of any real identity. What stuck with me was the younger woman, and how she seemed absent from any and all cultural features and individuality. She was a blank slate, a representation of something I've been noticing more and more: the death of authenticity.

The modern world is full of people adopting roles that aren't really theirs, taking on identities that don't quite fit. The younger waitress, with her oversized sweatshirt, could've been from any small town. She wasn't unique. The clothes she wore, the way she presented herself—it was all a uniform.

Everything you need to know about uniforms is in the name. They are designed to hide individuality, to make one indistinguishable from all. Modern culture is nothing more than a series of uniforms, where people take on symbols, styles, and behaviors that were never theirs to begin with, presenting themselves as part of something real when, in fact, it's nothing more than a simulation.

Everywhere I look, I hear Baudrillard's words—the echoes of simulacra and hyperreality growing louder with each passing day. His essays aren't just theoretical musings; they've become our reality. We live in a world of simulations, where the original is so deeply buried that it's impossible to find.

The world, whether we call it reality or simulation, is saturated with a lack of authenticity that is nearing critical mass, though there are still a few isolated places off the beaten path where it hasn't fully taken hold. But it's only a matter of time. I've said before that you can track the death of a culture by the loss of its accent and my ears seem only to hear the same dull inflections everywhere I go. And so, I find myself questioning what parts of our world are still genuine.

How does one distinguish what is real from what is just a simulation of something else? Even in my fiction, which is deeply influenced by the Southern Gothic tradition, I feel a lack of authenticity. I can't tap the same veins as Faulkner or O'Connor, and I'll never have McCarthy's depth, because the world they wrote about, the experiences they were rooted in, are alien to me, and we all know the old South died with air conditioning, so I'm just chasing ghosts.

But it's all too fast, we are physically and mentally transient, we are surrounded by non-places, non-ideas, non-concerns, and non-lives, that change before you have time to get your barring. True culture, the kind that grows organically, can't thrive when everything is constantly in flux. A forest becomes thick and deep because it has stood there, unchanged, for centuries. Trees don't reach great heights overnight, but we no longer give them time to grow. Our culture today is more like cheap pine—harvested quickly, sold off, and replaced with something artificial.

What this means is that people are navigating a world that feels less and less authentic. The entire world is turning into a giant gift shop—a place where things are sold to represent an idea of a place or culture that no longer exists if it ever did. It's Disney World, it's Epcot Center. Tennessee becomes a caricature of moonshiners and bootleggers slapped on a T-shirt. Where you can buy moonshine at the store, but it's not real moonshine. It can't be. It's packaged in a factory, slapped with a label, and sold at Manufacturer Suggested Retail Price, while they tell you it's something authentic when it's anything but.

That's the story of our world now. When you travel, you'll notice small differences in how modern culture is expressed, but at the end of the day, they're all the same. The variations are slight, it's Coke or Pepsi... it doesn't really matter. Both are just different flavors of the same garbage, designed to appeal to everyone and no one at the same time. The question of what's truly authentic is one I find myself grappling with constantly, but it's not one I expect to answer.

Every relationship, every song, every book, every TV show, movie, and news headline is manufactured to simulate something else, to create the illusion of authenticity that no longer exists.

What we're left with is copies, of copies, of copies, of copies, and we just want to believe if we dig deep enough, we will find something real.

[12]

Ghost Dancing in December

The great majority of people will go on observing forms that cannot be explained; they will keep Christmas Day with Christmas gifts and Christmas benedictions; they will continue to do it; and someday suddenly wake up and discover why.
– G.K. Chesterton, On Christmas.

As each holiday season approaches, I am increasingly aware of an emptiness, a sense of detachment from celebrations that once held meaning. Initially, I thought this was simply part of growing older—perhaps a natural fading of holiday magic. But I now believe that the holidays themselves have become Ghost Dances, hollow replicas disconnected from their origins.

For those unfamiliar, "Ghost Dancing" refers to a spiritual movement that swept through several Native American tribes in the late 1800s. The movement held that by practicing the Ghost Dance, believers could reunite with the spirits of their ancestors, who would aid in resisting American expansion.

The modern holiday season is in many ways a Ghost Dance in which Americans invoke lost cultural and spiritual traditions in an attempt to ward off the ever-increasing standardization of life.

The problem with any Ghost Dance is that it's inherently reactionary. It merely responds to the cultural decay that has already taken hold. Celebrating a holiday presupposes a sense of meaning, but the modern holiday season tries to create meaning through participation alone. This inversion—where participation is expected to produce significance—is what ultimately turns the holiday season into a Ghost Dance.

Most holidays we celebrate today have lost touch with their original cultural or religious significance. Take Halloween, for instance. It's so far removed from its roots that if you asked the average American about its origins, you'd be met with little more than vague references to Irish traditions or how they used to carve turnips instead of pumpkins. Any connection to All Hallows' Eve or All Saints Day will go unmentioned.

Thanksgiving, too, has suffered this fate. It is reduced to a conflict between two opposing sides. One side sees it as a celebration of a mythic harmony between Native Americans and pilgrims, while the other sees it as the glorification of the alleged genocide of Native Americans. In either case, Thanksgiving's origin and meaning are lost.

And then there's Christmas—the second most important holiday in Christianity, in which we celebrate the birth of our Lord, Jesus Christ. For most Americans, Christmas has largely become a secular event. Corporations have co-opted it, turning it into a consumerist spectacle centered around a commercialized Santa Claus and a diluted notion of gift-giving. The deeper, sacred meaning of the holiday is overshadowed by superficial customs and commercial interests.

The disconnect between the holidays and their origins is partly a consequence of America's increasing cultural diversity. Since 1964, the influx of cultures worldwide has diluted our long-standing traditions. While America never truly had a single monoculture, there were moments when a unified American ethos seemed possible, with European customs blending into something distinctly American.

Previously, immigrants shared certain cultural values—European holidays often centered around the celebration of Christian traditions that could easily be infused into the existing cultural Christianity of American society. The integration of these traditions helped create a semblance of shared heritage. But after 1964, the arrival of immigrants from cultures unfamiliar, and often opposed, to

Western Christianity led to a stripping down of religious elements from many holidays. Christmas, for instance, is harder to celebrate in its original form when it centers on Christ and the majority of new celebrants do not share that belief. Thus, the holiday has been increasingly secularized to ensure inclusivity, at the cost of meaning.

This dilution is also fueled by American capitalism's drive to commodify cultural rituals. For retailers, Christmas has become less about Jesus and more about maximizing sales, exchanging gifts, and generating profit. The commercialization of the holiday prioritizes its revenue potential, often at the expense of its deeper meaning. Santa Claus, for instance, is more profitable than the figure of Jesus; anything that boosts sales is magnified, while elements that can't be monetized are minimized or stripped away altogether.

Thanksgiving, for instance, resists commodification. It centers on a family meal and gratitude for what we already have, which doesn't lend itself to excessive spending. Consequently, Thanksgiving has nearly vanished from the retail landscape, overshadowed by the push to promote Christmas, a much more profitable holiday. Walk into any store the week of Halloween, and you'll see the spooky decorations swept aside to make way for Christmas displays, as the holiday season transforms into a commercial countdown.

Easter, though less commercialized than

Christmas, has also suffered a transformation. Originally a celebration of Christ's resurrection, Easter has been reduced to a holiday about the Easter Bunny and gift baskets. This distorted version is often wielded by atheists as an argument against Christianity's legitimacy, mistakenly linking Easter to ancient pagan worship of Ishtar, the Assyrian and Babylonian goddess of fertility. It is a stupid argument easily refuted by the fact that Easter, in most languages, is referred to as "Pascha" and is directly rooted in the Christian celebration of the resurrection.

In essence, our holidays have become Ghost Dances—attempts to cling to traditions that many no longer fully understand, while simultaneously trying to unite an increasingly diverse population.

The holidays have little power in a society no longer unified by shared cultural or religious values. Instead, we exist within a multiplicity of cultures, where meaningful traditions are diluted to avoid offending anyone. Thus, what remains are empty shells, simulations of what these holidays once represented.

This hollowness is something many of us feel instinctively. Yet, we continue to participate, putting on the mask, and going through the motions, because we need to. Humans need traditions; we crave meaning, connection, and a sense of belonging. So, even though the essence has been stripped away, we dance on.

If we wish to turn our holidays into more than a Ghost Dance, we must make an intentional effort to reconnect with their origins. Thanksgiving can again become a time of gratitude for what we have and a celebration of the American origins, Halloween can be reconnected to All Saints' Day. Christmas can once more focus on the birth of Christ. In our homes, we have the power to honor the true essence of these celebrations.

The secular versions of these holidays will eventually fade, precisely because they lack substance. When times get hard, people do not cling to empty rituals; they hold fast to beliefs and traditions that have real meaning. Those who remember the deeper significance of these holidays will carry them forward, celebrating Christmas as the birth of Christ, Easter as the resurrection, and Thanksgiving as a time for gratitude. Meanwhile, the commercialized, empty, rootless versions will vanish in time.

When I see the commercial machine don the "skin suit" of our traditions, I take solace in knowing that these superficial versions cannot last. Built on the shifting sands of consumerism, they lack the foundation necessary to endure. Appealing to everyone means ultimately appealing to no one. It is in small, dedicated communities that the heart of these holidays will endure, carrying forward the true spirit that gives life and purpose to our celebrations.

[13]

Modern Marriage & Modern Lies

One of the most renowned passages in the Bible, Matthew 6:24, conveys Christ's message that one cannot serve two masters. While it primarily highlights the perils of attempting to serve both God and material wealth, this verse can also be interpreted more broadly to address various aspects of life. Lately, Pearl Davis has ignited a controversy by urging young men to refrain from marriage. This provocative suggestion has naturally sparked significant backlash from online right-wing circles and mainstream conservatives alike. Talking heads like Ben Shapiro and Matt Walsh have vehemently criticized her viewpoint, insisting that marriage is a noble institution and young men should be encouraged to embrace it.

As a happily, married man myself, I

wholeheartedly endorse and recognize the numerous advantages and significance of the institution of marriage. Throughout history, the family has been considered a microcosm of society – affectionately known as "the little commonwealth" – with its stability governed by the harmonious union of husband and wife. Indeed, marriage represents the bedrock upon which the entire family structure is built.

Be that as it may, this doesn't imply that Pearl's critique holds no merit. It is undeniably evident that contemporary marriage has evolved into more of a legal obligation that disproportionately bestows benefits upon women. Without delving into every minute detail, aspects such as divorce proceedings, custody battles, alimony payments, and child support arrangements tend to be predominantly advantageous to women. Consequently, it should come as no surprise that individuals like Pearl and a growing number of young men view marriage as an uphill battle with insurmountable odds stacked against them. Why would someone willingly enter into an agreement where only one party will reap substantial benefits?

With this perspective in mind, while we must respect the sanctity of marriage and its ability to foster close-knit families and stable societies, we must also remain open to valid critiques. Acknowledging these challenges surrounding modern-day marriages allows us to work towards a solution and offer men and women real-world advice.

Naturally, individuals like Shapiro vehemently challenge Pearl's perspective, offering retorts akin to the relational equivalent of "vote harder." Their advice consists of getting married, embracing religious beliefs, finding the perfect partner, and so on. As one would expect from today's mainstream conservatives, these suggestions may seem valuable on the surface; however, they tend to either actively or subconsciously overlook the crux of the issue.

The inherent fallacy among modern conservatives often lies in their failure to recognize their own indoctrination with liberal ideals. Unwittingly absorbing 90% of these concepts while attempting to advocate traditional values. The stark reality is that true traditionalism cannot coexist with liberal egalitarian philosophy. One cannot accept the tenets of modern feminism while at the same time trying to encourage traditional values. They are oil and water.

By developing a more comprehensive understanding of this ideological inconsistency and addressing it head-on, modern conservatives can present a stronger and more authoritative argument on the compatibility between traditionalism and select aspects of liberalism, but don't hold your breath.

The amusing paradox we find ourselves discussing is that if one were to genuinely embrace feminism for its core principle – the idea that women should be treated with absolute equality to men – then numerous gender-related issues would likely vanish. Custody battles wouldn't see women emerging victorious every single time, they wouldn't automatically retain the house, and they couldn't walk away from a relationship "simply because the spark isn't there any longer." Regrettably, it seems that taking responsibility for one's actions isn't a trait commonly associated with feminists. As such, losing every custody battle isn't high on the wish list for most women either, which as the 20th century has shown means that women (feminist or not) struggle to grasp the true consequences of their own ideology.

This leaves us at a fascinating crossroads: you must either dismiss feminism in its entirety – encompassing every aspect from women in the workplace to higher education and even female sports – or you must wholeheartedly embrace feminism in its purest form. This would involve replacing each and every law and standard that grants special treatment to women, exchanging them with rules based on genuine equality.

In considering the matter of gender equality, two main perspectives often surface: either women are equal to men, or they remain in a subordinate position. If we embrace the former notion, it is only fair that women are treated as such. However, if we lean towards the latter belief, it becomes crucial to provide special treatment for women in order to ensure their safety and well-being. Unfortunately, one cannot eat their cake and have it too. Public figures like Shapiro and Walsh, along with numerous conservative pundits, find themselves caught in a paradoxical web – as much as they want to deny it, they are essentially a throwback to liberals from two decades ago.

That said, we must now shift our focus toward the crux of this debate: the overarching influence of liberal egalitarianism coloring our world. Ultimately, what lies at the heart of this struggle is a choice between the principles of tradition and those of liberalism. None of us – myself included – have escaped being born into a world permeated with various degrees of egalitarianism. Consequently, rejecting this mindset may seem utterly unattainable given the current culture. Nevertheless, if one truly wishes to mend societal issues related to marriage and gender roles, there is no room for half-measures; a wholehearted commitment becomes imperative.

It is crucial that each individual choose their allegiance: either serve liberal egalitarian values or uphold traditional ones. In doing so, we arrive at something that looks like horseshoe theory – you can either follow feminism to its ultimate conclusion or dismiss it completely; there is no middle ground on which to stand. It's a zero-sum game.

[14]

The Scent of Postmodernism

Recently, I had the opportunity to rewatch the film *Scent of a Woman.*[11] If you haven't seen it, it stars Al Pacino as Frank Slade, a retired Army Lieutenant Colonel who, due to a tragic military accident, has lost his sight. The movie explores the ethical dilemma of suicide, all within the backdrop of a postmodern context. The film tries to squeeze some value from human life in a world absent of any metaphysical belief.

As the story unfolds, we discover that Frank Slade has made the decision to end his own life, after experiencing a weekend of indulgence in the vibrant city of New York. When confronted by Charlie Simms, a compassionate prep school student played by Chris O'Donnell, Frank asks for a reason to keep on living. In response, all Charlie can muster are two weak materialistic commodities. He highlights

Frank's remarkable skills in tango dancing and driving a Ferrari, suggesting that these simple pleasures are what make life worth living. Frank, I know life is hard but hey, you sure can dance. It's genuinely convincing.

In a different era, Frank Slade might have received guidance reminiscent of George Bailey's in It's a *Wonderful Life.*[12] Perhaps a guardian angel or a wise priest would have shown him the beauty and significance of life, helping him rediscover his purpose and the positive impact he can still make in the world. However, in the film's 1992 setting, material luxuries seem to take center stage as the ultimate source of fulfillment and happiness. This reduction of life's worth to materialism aligns with the decline of meta-narratives, a crucial aspect of postmodernism.

From a traditional Christian perspective, this reductionist approach to the value of life raises concerns about the impact of postmodernism on ethical discourse. Catholic teachings emphasize the intrinsic dignity and sanctity of every human life, rooted in the belief that life is a precious gift from God.[13] By reducing life's worth to worldly pleasures, "Scent of a Woman" undermines this fundamental principle, neglecting the deeper philosophical and moral dimensions that have historically guided ethical deliberation within Catholic thought.

Postmodernism, influenced by thinkers such as Jean Baudrillard, Jean-François Lyotard, and Charles

Jencks, challenges the traditional Catholic understanding of objective moral values rooted in natural law and divine revelation. Baudrillard argues that in a hyperreal society, where simulacra and signs replace reality, the boundaries between the real and the imaginary blur, leading to a loss of meaning and a sense of emptiness.[14] In his work *The Postmodern Condition*, Lyotard asserts that postmodernism is characterized by skepticism toward grand narratives and fragmentation of knowledge, resulting in a multiplicity of language games and localized truths.[15] Jencks, in *The Language of Post-Modern Architecture*, explores how postmodernism challenges modernist ideals by embracing pastiche, irony, and historical references.[16]

From a Christian perspective, the rejection of universal moral truths and the fragmentation of truth advocated by postmodernism can lead to moral relativism, where ethical standards become purely subjective and contingent upon individual preferences and societal norms. Catholicism, on the other hand, asserts that there are objective moral truths that transcend individual perspectives and cultural relativism. The Catholic moral framework, guided by natural law and the teachings of the Church, provides a solid foundation for addressing complex ethical dilemmas, such as suicide, by recognizing the inherent worth and purpose of human life and the call to love and care for one another.

Furthermore, the film's emphasis on materialistic pleasures reflects the broader cultural influence of postmodernism, which often promotes consumerism and a self-centered mindset. For Christians, life's meaning and fulfillment extend beyond pursuing transient pleasures and material wealth. Catholic teachings emphasize the importance of self-sacrifice, virtuous living, and the pursuit of spiritual goods as essential elements of a meaningful life.[17]

In evaluating the deeply flawed ethical dilemmas depicted in *Scent of a Woman*, it becomes evident that the pervasive influence of postmodernism, as propagated by the likes of Baudrillard, Lyotard, and Jencks, represents a dangerous assault on traditional values and moral foundations. The relentless rejection of universal moral truths and the deliberate fragmentation of truth characteristic of postmodern thought serves as a corrosive force, corroding the very essence of human dignity and undermining the sanctity of life championed by Catholic teachings.

The film's lamentable emphasis on materialistic hedonism and the pursuit of selfish pleasures epitomizes the hollow and empty ethos fostered by postmodernism, callously disregarding the profound spiritual and moral dimensions that have historically guided ethical discourse within the Catholic/ Christian tradition. It is an imperative duty to vehemently criticize the pernicious influence of postmodernism, resolutely upholding the enduring principles of Christianity, deeply rooted in natural law and divine revelation, which alone offer a solid foundation for meaningful ethical deliberation and the preservation of the intrinsic worth of every human being.

[15]

Bootstrap Theology and Realpolitik

Once a month, my Twitter feed gets hijacked by a video featuring a young woman with tears in her eyes expressing dissatisfaction with the crucible of the 40-hour workweek. The complaints are consistently repetitive, revolving around the stress of working 40 hours, commuting, and managing a household. In the most Pavlovian manner, conservatives, predominantly Boomers and old Gen-Xers respond with accusations of laziness, entitlement, and the evergreen mention of "Bootstraps." This is an uncharitable and selfish response, without an ounce of self-awareness and one that does little more than help to alienate young people from the conservative movement, and no one embodies this ton-deaf reaction better than Matt Walsh.

As usual, Matt Walsh fails to comprehend why Zoomers are dissatisfied with the labor market. He merely perceives a lazy and entitled individual who seemingly refuses to work. There is no effort on his part to understand the underlying reasons for her discontent or why she might feel the way she does. He expects her to be content with five hours of free time each day, not to mention weekends.

Now, let's assume that Matt Walsh genuinely feels this way and is not being a disingenuous liar. Let's examine what all this purported free time looks like.

Let's assume, for the sake of argument, that the young woman is married and has one child, with a one-hour round-trip daily commute. If she works from 8 am to 5 pm, she leaves the house around 7 am and returns around 6 pm, depending on the time it takes to pick up her children. This leaves her with about five hours in her day. During these five hours, she and her husband must prepare dinner, assist with homework, handle dishes, start laundry, get the kids ready for bed, pack lunches, and take showers. In reality, she has perhaps one hour, depending on how much sleep she desires.

"But don't worry," Matt says, "You have the weekend." In reality, her weekend is consumed by catching up on all the housework that she couldn't manage during the week, making it a little better than the workweek itself.

Now surely Matt would say that she could just not work, that her husband should sustain their family on his income alone. The truth is that a dual-income household is almost a necessity for the vast majority of Americans. I am not going to address the offshoring of jobs, inflation, immigration, or any number of other factors that make it nearly impossible for American families to live on a single income. The point of all of this is to draw attention to the fact that conservatives are tone-deaf spiritual boomers who fail to address the complaints of young people and then act shocked when they all vote blue.

The response to all of this from Matt Walsh and his ilk will likely be to blame the Democrats but the truth is that they are no more guilty than Republicans.

I do not think that there is any political solution to our current problems, but that does not change the fact that you need grassroots support, you need the favor of the people, the mandate of heaven if you will. Bismark understood this, he understood realpolitik.

During the socialist revolutions that spread across Europe in the late 19th century, Bismarck saw the writing on the wall. He didn't ignore the complaints of the working class. Instead, he introduced Staatssozialismus— a series of reforms that addressed the complaints of the working class. This was a calculated move on the part of Bismark that satisfied the workers and cut the legs out from under the Social Democratic Party of Germany. As it turns out most workers weren't socialists, rather they were dissatisfied with the current state of affairs and the socialists were the only ones willing to listen. Bismark addressed their most basic grievances and in doing so halted the socialist movement in Germany.

Setting aside debates on the enduring impact of Bismarck's reforms, the sway of realpolitik remains undeniable. Young people possess legitimate reasons for discontent with the current status quo, and conservatives who dismiss them do so at their peril. Adopting the stance of spiritual Boomers risks further alienating a generation in search of understanding and concrete solutions.

A wise statesman will not try to impose his ideas upon the people but will look attentively at what the people want and make them believe that they want it too.

– Otto Von Bismarck

The response from Matt Walsh and his associates underscores their blindness to the reality on the ground and their unwillingness to take others' complaints seriously. The system is unsustainable, and Zoomers act as canaries in the coal mine; their signals are ignored by conservatives while the left merely pays them lip service. This is an opportune moment to address the grievances of young workers and provide pragmatic solutions, practicing some realpolitik.

[16]

Circling The Drain with Cthulhu

When Disney acquired the Star Wars franchise in 2012, it appeared to be a golden ticket. Here was a multi-billion-dollar franchise that was guaranteed to be profitable with minimal maintenance. Star Wars had survived the lackluster prequels and was able to maintain cultural relevance with little more than six films and a handful of video games for nearly 40 years.

Disney didn't even need to create new stories; all they had to do was adapt the hundreds of stories that filled the Star Wars novelized canon. Despite being handed a money-printing IP, Disney managed to fumble the ball. They turned a guaranteed win into a loss in record time. At first glance, this would appear to be a colossal business failure. However, Disney repeated the same series of mistakes with the

Marvel franchise. Another IP with an extensive back catalog that only needed to be maintained, another money printer.

Yet, both franchises have seen declining box office returns, dwindling merchandise sales, and waning cultural relevance under Disney's stewardship. The reason for this failure is obvious. It doesn't take an MBA to recognize that Disney's focus on DEI and "wokeness" killed two golden calves. Anyone with a room temperature IQ should have noticed that the more DEI-driven each film or show became, the worse its return on investment. Yet, She persisted.

A closer examination of the funding mechanisms behind left-wing media and DEI initiatives is quite telling. Information from DataRepubican.com[18] shows that a significant portion of funding for these initiatives comes from the government, funneled through taxpayer dollars and USAID. This creates a closed-loop system where the left uses taxpayer money to fund woke media, which is then consumed primarily by the left. It's a self-sustaining cycle, a dog eating its own vomit in perpetuity.

Noam Chomsky's concept of "manufactured consent" describes how institutions shape public opinion to align with the interests of the powerful, and this closed-loop reveals a critical flaw in the manufacturing of consent. As we all know the internet has shattered the monopoly on information that the regime once held, but it has also had a second, unintended effect: it has turned manufactured consent in on itself.

The regime's patronage network prioritizes hiring loyalists, who then reinforce the regime's ideology. As these loyalists rise through the ranks, they become further entrenched in the system, creating companies staffed entirely by true believers. What the USAID data reveals is that these regime loyalists are also the primary consumers of regime propaganda. They are insulated from reality, living in a bubble where their beliefs are constantly reaffirmed.

When a Star Wars film flops, they don't see it as a failure of their ideology; they see it as an anomaly, a sign that their ideas need to be enforced more aggressively. This feedback loop creates a disconnect between the creators of media and the broader audience and solidifies the idea that more propaganda is needed.

Disney's failure with Star Wars and Marvel is a prime example of this breakdown in consent manufacturing. The left has captured institutions to such an extent that they have created a closed-loop system, speed-running DEI initiatives while the rest of the world watches in bewilderment. They cannot understand how Trump won in 2016, and they cannot comprehend why Star Wars fans reject lesbian space witches.

At the same, the internet has also accelerated the speed at which propaganda is produced and consumed. The regime's loyalists being trapped in an internal DEI arms race have been producing and consuming propaganda at an unprecedented pace. Trapped in this self-referencing world they can't help but push Overton Window at maximum velocity.

You can't speedrun propaganda. The gay rights movement took nearly 40 years to normalize gay marriage, and even then, the average American is tolerant at best. The left has been driving cultural change at Mach-10 for a decade leaving little room for the average person to adjust their beliefs.

Effective propaganda is like concrete; it needs time to settle. The internet works against this, as the slow and steady dissemination of ideas is antithetical to the digital age. Trapped in their self-created cultural prison, the left has failed to realize that they are the only consumers of their own delusions. Cthulhu swam left too fast and is now trapped in a whirlpool of his own creation and everyone else is just watching.

When we see Democrats doubling down on the same tired rhetoric and ideas it because that's all they know. It's Plato's cave on full display. This is why Auron MacIntyre is correct that the woke can't be put away, they are trapped and nothing short of an ideological lobotomy will fix that. Don't expect the left to change tactics, they can't, they're trapped and we should do what we can to make that cave stays sealed.

[17]

Anonymity and Alienation: The Cultural Impact of Non-Places

Children learn primarily through observation. From the moment they open their eyes, the world is an infinite expanse of the unknown, and they rely on those around them to navigate this new territory. By observing their surroundings, children mimic the actions and behaviors of the people closest to them. Walking, talking, eating, and playing—nearly everything is absorbed through careful observation and imitation.

Though adults may step in to correct a word's pronunciation or demonstrate how to properly hold a fork, the initial attempts at these activities stem from observing the family's social norms and rituals. The home, then, becomes the central hub of learning. It is where children feel most at ease, where interactions flow seamlessly, and where understanding often requires no explanation. The comfort of home is built on shared knowledge—both conscious and unconscious—of how things are and how they will unfold. This familiarity, established over time, creates a deep sense of belonging.

The patterns, people, and places within the home and surrounding community are understood without question. From these spaces, we derive a sense of identity. The language we speak, the clothes we wear, and the customs we follow are all rooted in the shared experiences that come from growing up in a particular environment.

Time, however, is the key element that transforms a house into a home. It is time that allows the unpredictable to become predictable, where even unexpected events fit within a larger, familiar pattern. Without the passage of time, a home is just another space, indistinct and transient. Home becomes a non-place without time—a space where one remains a stranger, moving through without connection.

This concept of "non-places" was introduced by French anthropologist Marc Augé in *Non-Places: Introduction to an Anthropology of Supermodernity*.[19] Augé observed that modern society is increasingly filled with spaces devoid of identity, history, or personal connection. As globalization, technological advancement, and consumerism accelerate, these non-places shape how we interact with the world and define our sense of belonging.

Non-Places and the Erosion of Meaning

Everything proceeds as if space had been trapped by time, as if there were no history other than the last forty-eight hours of news, as if each individual history were drawing its motives, its words, and images, from the inexhaustible stock of an unending history in the present.
-Marc Auge

Augé characterizes non-places as spaces where individuals become anonymous, where human connection fades, and where personal histories hold no meaning. Spaces like airports, highways, hotel chains, and supermarkets are the quintessential non-places. These environments are designed for function, not for fostering community or meaning. They are spaces we move through but never truly inhabit.

How many times have you been sitting in an airport, surrounded by thousands of people? Despite the crowd, there is a pervasive sense of isolation. Everyone is in transit, focused only on getting from one point to the next. There are no shared histories or connections between the individuals passing through. This place, the airport, becomes the archetypal non-place—a transient, impersonal space built for efficiency and movement.

The birth of the non-place is a direct consequence of what Augé calls supermodernity—a product of our globalized, hyper-connected, fast-paced world. In this world, we are constantly on the move, and non-places multiply. Every city and every country is increasingly dominated by these same spaces—standardized, impersonal, and efficient. This homogenization erodes the assortment of experiences that once defined the places we inhabited.

The Contrast Between Non-Places and Places

The character is at home when he is at ease in the rhetoric of the people with whom he shares life. The sign of being at home is the ability to make oneself understood without too much difficulty, and to follow the reasoning of others without any need for long explanations.

-Marc Auge

In contrast to non-places, meaningful places are imbued with identity, relationships, and history. Places like a small rural town, your family home, or church carry deep personal and cultural significance. These are spaces where human connection thrives, where memories are formed, and where individuals experience a sense of belonging.

The distinction between place and non-place highlights a deeper, existential issue. In traditional places, people feel "at home" not just because of the physical space, but because of the shared language, culture, and experiences that bind them to the community. As Augé notes, being "at home" means being understood with little effort and understanding others without the need for long explanations. There is an unspoken, shared vocabulary that fosters both comfort and connection.

Non-places, on the other hand, strip away this sense of belonging. They are generic spaces, designed for everyone and no one. They facilitate movement and consumption, but they do not encourage attachment or personal connection. The very nature of non-places makes it difficult, if not impossible, to form lasting bonds.

If a place can be defined as relational, historical and concerned with identity, then a space which cannot be defined as relation, or historical, or concerned with identity will be a non-place. The hypothesis advanced here is that supermodernity produces non-places, meaning spaces that are not themselves anthropological places and which, unlike Baudelairean modernity, do not integrate the earlier places: instead, these are listed, classified, promoted to the status of 'places of memory', and assigned to a circumscribed and specific position. A world where people are born in the clinic and die in hospital, where transit points and temporary abodes are proliferating under luxurious or inhuman conditions -Marc Auge

The Threat to Cultural Identity

The most insidious consequence of the rise of non-places is the threat they pose to cultural identity. Augé argues that non-places are a by-product of globalization and the "cultural acid of standardization." This process erodes the unique cultural markers that once distinguished different regions, communities, and individuals. Whether you find yourself in New York, Dallas, or a small town, walking into a chain store or a fast-food restaurant feels the same. The homogenized experience strips away any sense of regional character or cultural distinctiveness.

This cultural erosion is a serious problem for societies increasingly disconnected from their historical roots and regional identities. Without spaces that foster human connection, tradition, and shared experiences, communities lose their unique cultural fabric, and individuals struggle to find meaning in their surroundings.

Alienation and Anonymity in Non-Places

Living in a world dominated by non-places fosters a sense of alienation and anonymity. In non-places, human interactions are superficial or entirely absent. You may pass by hundreds of people in a shopping mall or an airport, but none of them are truly present. Each person is engaged in their own isolated experience, disconnected from the others around them.

This sense of anonymity is overpowering, especially in a world that is supposedly more connected than ever through technology. Despite the rise of social media and global communication, the physical spaces we inhabit often leave us feeling more isolated and disconnected than ever before. Non-places thus become emblematic of the paradox of modern life: we are more connected than ever, yet more alone.

Reclaiming Meaningful Spaces

In response to the spread of non-places, Augé's work suggests that we must reclaim and prioritize spaces that foster human connection and cultural identity. We need places where individuals can feel a sense of belonging, where they can form relationships and create lasting memories.

The design of public spaces, homes, and communities should emphasize more than just functionality. These spaces should encourage interaction, creativity, and shared experience. Efficiency alone is not worth the loss of cultural meaning and human connection. If we continue to prioritize non-places, we will lose our sense of identity and community.

As globalization and technological advancement continue to accelerate, non-places will only multiply.

The challenge for modern society is to resist this trend and to cultivate environments that support human connection, cultural identity, and a sense of belonging. In a world increasingly defined by transit and consumption, we must remember the importance of place—the spaces that shape who we are and where we belong. Only by reclaiming these meaningful places can we find our way back home.

[18]

Marxism and the Modern Right: A Complex Legacy

It's nearly impossible to engage with 20th-century thinkers without encountering the influence of Marx. For many on the political right, even acknowledging Marx's contributions can feel like heresy. Yet, dismissing Marx outright without understanding his impact and the context of his ideas would be a mistake. To grasp why Marxism and other utopian ideologies gained traction during the turn of the century, it is important to understand the historical disruptions that shaped his thought and the subsequent integration of his ideas into various intellectual traditions, including those of his critics.

Historical Context

Karl Marx and Friedrich Engels were writing during

a time of massive change. The Industrial Revolution disrupted the very fabric of human society. Before the Industrial Revolution, a man could provide for himself and his family through his labor. He could work the land or take up a small trade, and this would be enough to get by. After the Industrial Revolution, man could no longer survive by his labor but rather by selling his labor. Large portions of the population were forced into factories, enduring horrendous working conditions. Many, though not all, factory owners (bourgeoisie) were extremely exploitative. When Marx complained about children getting crushed to death in factories, it was because it was actually happening. The Industrial Revolution was brutal and disturbing for many, and Marx provided a solution.

Marxism is fundamentally materialist (dialectical and historical), focusing on economic relations and class struggle as the driving forces of historical change. Orthodox Marxism advocates for the overthrow of capitalist systems and the establishment of a classless society. Most of this did not concern the average worker, who cared more about their living conditions than dialectical materialism.

Influence on The Right

There are strong undertones of Marxist thought in many right-wing thinkers including Sam Francis and

James Burnham. Sam Francis, as a paleoconservative, did not advocate for the abolition of capitalism but rather criticized the distortions he perceived within it, particularly those brought by globalism and the managerial state. Francis's analyses involved a critique of the ruling elite. While Marx focused on the bourgeoisie as the capitalist class exploiting the proletariat, Francis was concerned with the "managerial elite" or "New Class," who he saw as controlling modern bureaucratic and corporate institutions.

James Burnham's intellectual trajectory is an example of a thinker who transitioned from Marxism to a form of conservatism that included elements of managerial theory and geopolitical realism. His early work was influenced by Marxist thought, but his later theories represented a significant departure from Marx, focusing on the rise of a managerial elite and rejecting key Marxist principles such as historical materialism and the inevitability of proletarian revolution. Burnham's work is thus a complex blend of initial Marxist influence and subsequent conservative evolution. His seminal work, *The Managerial Revolution*, posited that a new class of managers, not the proletariat, would come to dominate the socio-economic landscape, a view that diverged sharply from Marx.

Modern Class Dynamics

The managerial class that dominates our current age can be seen as rule by the bourgeoisie. There is little difference between the bourgeois/merchant class and the managerial elite. Both are driven by the accumulation of capital and are willing to exploit the working class to maximize efficiency and increase their power. This working class vs. managerial elite conflict is, in many ways, an updated version of the bourgeoisie vs. the proletariat, at the end of the day they are simply different manifestations of class conflict.

Class Resentment and Solutions

Both the early adopters of Marxism and the current online right are driven, in part, by class resentment. For some, this means they see themselves as disaffected elites, and while this is fanciful at best, they are in the minority. The majority, much like the Russian factory workers at the turn of the century, simply wanted a less oppressive and exploitative bourgeoisie or, in our case, a managerial class.

Marxists want to see the means of production turned over to the unwashed masses. This doesn't work and never will. Those on the right understand this, and as a result, our solution is a return to a properly ordered class structure. Hierarchy is crucial to the right-wing conception of the world. We understand that class exists whether you want it to or not. The means of production should not be seized and given to the workers. Rather, their control should be handed to a proper aristocracy that prioritizes something other than efficiency and profit. In short, the Marxist wants the destruction of class, and the right wants a responsible and properly ordered class.

In the end, it is important that we understand that while we reject Marx as the vindictive, jealous loser that he was, we also recognize that his critiques were often responding to the legitimate problems of his day. Because of this, many of our most beloved thinkers were either former Marxists or touched with the Marxist brush. They carried the residue of class conflict with them, it's in their framing and their language, and it has, in many ways, infused itself into our thoughts as well. We should recognize the Marxist tendencies within our thoughts (as small as they might be) so that we may properly address the problems of our day and turn a tendency toward class warfare into class restoration.

[19]

The Church

[20]

The End of Christendom

> *First of all, we are at the end of Christendom, now not Christianity, not the Church. Remember what I am saying. – Archbishop Fulton Sheen*

In 1974, Archbishop Fulton Sheen declared that we were in the beginning stages of the 4th great crisis of the Church, the end of Christendom, the end of, "the economic, political, and social life as inspired by Christian principles.

We are living in the fourth five-hundred-year period of Church history. And the Church is not a continuing thing. It dies and [rises] again. It proceeds on the principle of Christ himself as priest and victim. We go along for a while and we die, like the serpent, we shed our skin, like nature itself we shed our leaves, and there comes a defeat, seeing decay, we're put in the grave, and then we rise again.

Archbishop Sheen, (inspired in part by Toynbee) believed there were four deaths in the Church's history.

The first death was the fall of Rome. "Rome had become Christian. There were martyrs and saints for two centuries or more, and after Rome became Christian, barbarians from without came in and destroyed Rome, and she fell as nothing has fallen since Satan fell from the heavens."

The second decay began around the year 1000 with the Muslim invasions. "The Muslims swept within 120 miles of Paris, the great battle of Poitiers, and then they came around, formed a crescent, and came up to the gates of Vienna." The rise of Islam was a precursor to the second death: the Great Schism, "The schism of Constantinople, in which the church was split, and it seemed to be the end of everything. But again, the Church was reborn."

Decadence and decay brought the third death, "when the Church became rotten, when nuns began defecting, priests began defecting, the pontiffs were not good. The Church seemed at an end. Then the Reformers came, but the Reformers almost always reform the wrong thing. They began reforming the Faith. There was nothing wrong with faith. It was the morals that needed to be reformed."

We are now in the midst of the 4th death, "We're spoiled. No great zeal, no great learning, no great fire, we're just against things, so often. What is the attack today? "Today, we have to conform to the world, or we're branded. Our Lord said, "Satan will sift you as wheat," and we're being sifted as wheat."

Our modern crisis is one of meaning, of authenticity, of purpose. We live in a world of illusions, or as Baudrillard put it, "Hyperreality." The screen shows us a world that is more real than real. Women are bombarded with images of something that cannot be, men are sold heroes greater in body and lesser in spirit then men of the past, boys are sold adventures, played with joysticks, no sacrifice required. The world has filled our bellies and emptied our souls.

So, we search for meaning, for something real. Many turn to empty pleasures, material gain, physical and emotional highs. Temporary fixes, band aids treating the symptoms, and neglecting the disease.

Those that turn to the Church, what do they find? Pastors and priests that preach the gospel of the world. A Christianity that molds itself to the sin of the day. They offer excuses and rationalization for all of man's faults. The result, a dying church, a dying faith, but we should not fear.

Archbishop Sheen saw an opportunity in this.

"Now, we can say aye or nay. We can bear up under assault, criticism, and ridicule because this is the love of Christians in the days of the Spirit of the World. It is not a gloomy picture. It is a picture of the Church in the midst of increasing opposition from the world. Therefore, live your lives in full consciousness of this, our testament, and rally close to the heart of Christ."

As the Church declines in number, it will grow in the faithful. The true believers will fill the pews. From the true believers a new evangelization will be born. For us this means we must hold strong to the faith, truth in the Lord, and lead those close to us toward the truth.

The same power that raised Christ from the dead is living in you. – Romans 8:11

[21]

You're called to be meek. That doesn't mean what you think it does.

The knight is a man of blood and iron, a man familiar with the sight of smashed faces and the ragged stumps of lopped-off limbs; he is also a demure, almost maidenlike, guest in a hall, a gentle, modest, unobtrusive man. He is not compromise or happy mean between ferocity and meekness; he is fierce to the nth and meek to the nth. The man who combines both characters – the knight – is not a work of nature but of art; of that art which has human beings, instead of canvas or marble, for its medium.
— C.S. Lewis, The Necessity of Chivalry

A false understanding of meekness has left us wandering and confused. Christians have experienced the removal of prayer from schools, have observed the erection of satanic statues in public spaces, and have been coerced into compromising their beliefs.

This retreat has filled many Christians with righteous anger, only to be met by pastors and priests advising passivity, claiming there is little to be done but to watch as evil flourishes. This call for inaction is often justified by a misinterpretation of the Christian virtue of meekness. Meekness, however, is not about passive acceptance of wrongdoing.

Instead, it signifies *controlled strength and humility*, much like the well-trained war horses of ancient Greece, powerful yet disciplined, ready to act with wisdom and courage.

To understand meekness, we must first explore its origin. The word "meek" is often misinterpreted as weakness or docility, but its true meaning is far more profound.

Our modern word 'meek' finds its origin in the Old Norse word *mjukr,* which means "soft, pliant, gentle."[20] 'Gentle' – the counterpart of meek – is derived from the Old French *gentil/jentil* which means, "high-born, worthy, noble, of good family; courageous, valiant; fine, good, fair."[21] Already, we see an interesting contrast emerge between the two terms. This contrast is indicative of the underlying complexity; neither of these words fully captures the Greek term used in Scripture.

In Greek, the word translated as meek, and gentle is πραΰς (*praus*). We find the word "praus," used four times in the New Testament (Matt 5:5; 11:29; 21:5; 1 Pet 3:4):

Blessed are the meek, for they will inherit the earth. – Matthew 5:5

Take my yoke upon you, and learn from me; for I am gentle and humble in heart, and you will find rest for your souls. – Matthew 11:29

Tell the daughter of Zion, Look, your king is coming to you, gentle, and mounted on a donkey, and on a colt, the foal of a donkey." – Matthew 21:5

Rather, let your adornment be the inner self with the lasting beauty of a gentle and quiet spirit, which is very precious in God's sight." – 1 Peter 3:4

Xenophon, the ancient Greek historian, wrote The Art of Horsemanship around 355 BC. This was a time of transition on the Greek battlefield: a traditional reliance on hoplites was being challenged by increasingly excellent horsemen, particularly from Thessaly.

The Art of Horsemanship served as a manual for newly important questions regarding the selection and training of warhorses. Xenophon describes the ideal cavalry horse as:

The horse that is sound in his feet, gentle and fairly

speedy, has the will and the strength to stand work, and, above all, is obedient.[22]

Xenophon uses the same word found in the New Testament, "gentle," πραΰς (*praus*), which is rooted in the word πρᾳότης (*praotēs*), defined as displaying the right blend of force and reserve (gentleness). A more direct translation of praotēs would be "strength under control" or "one who avoids unnecessary harshness without compromising or being too slow to use necessary force."

For the Greeks, a *praus* animal was one that had been trained and domesticated and was completely under control. There is no value in a warhorse that is weak, but rather one that can withstand the chaos of war while keeping its head, reserving its strength for the proper moment so as to turn the tide of battle.

The early church had a complete understanding of what it meant for Christians to be meek. St. Ambrose writes:

Soften therefore your temper that you be not angry, at least that you be angry, and sin not. It is a noble thing to govern passion by reason; nor is it a less virtue to check anger, than to be entirely without anger, since one is esteemed the sign of a weak, the other of a strong, mind.[23]

In the *Summa,* St. Thomas Aquinas concurs regarding the view of meekness as a rational restraint on anger:

Consequently meekness, in so far as it restrains the onslaught of anger, concurs with clemency towards the same effect; yet they differ from one another, inasmuch as clemency moderates external punishment, while meekness properly mitigates the passion of anger.[24]

There is no better example of meekness in its totality than Christ himself, who exemplifies strength under control throughout the Gospels. Christ demonstrates the proper use of righteous anger when he chases the moneylenders out of the temple:

In the temple he found people selling cattle, sheep, and doves and the money changers seated at their tables. Making a whip of cords, he drove all of them out of the temple, with the sheep and the cattle. He also poured out the coins of the money changers and overturned their tables. – John 2:13-16

Christ's response to those defiling his Father's house is one of meekness. He does not rush into the temple when he hears words of what is taking place. Rather he takes his time braiding a whip and when he is done he enters the temple and turns over the tables and chases the money lenders from the grounds. Once they flee, he does not give chase or find them later on and enact vengeance. While confronting those responsible he uses only the amount of force necessary to clear them out and rectify the situation.

We see the other side of meekness in Christ when the Roman soldiers come to take him away.

When Jesus' followers saw what was going to happen, they said, "Lord, should we strike with our swords?" And one of them struck the servant of the high priest, cutting off his right ear. But Jesus answered, "No more of this!" And he touched the man's ear and healed him.

-Luke 22:49-51

Here, Christ exemplifies meekness through restraint, discerning that the situation does not warrant the use of force. Rather than reacting impulsively, he chooses the path of peace deliberately. His response stands in stark contrast to the disciples, who react with quick anger and violence, drawing swords and injuring a Roman soldier. Christ intervenes, instructing them to cease their actions, and proceeds to compassionately heal the wounded soldier, willingly submitting to capture.

In both instances, we witness the embodiment of Christian meekness in Christ's demeanor. His actions are far from indicative of frailty, fear, or weakness. When necessary, he acts with calculated resolve; when restraint and peaceful submission are appropriate, he demonstrates humility and self-control.

This portrayal of praus, as described by both Xenophon and Aristotle, underscores that meekness is not synonymous with weakness or passivity. Rather, it is a manifestation of righteous anger – a controlled and purposeful response. Therefore, meekness is not indifference, timidity, or acquiescence, but rather a strength tempered by ethical discernment and spiritual grounding.

Thou wert the meekest man, says Sir Ector to the dead Launcelot. Thou wert the meekest man that ever ate in hall among ladies; and thou wert the sternest knight to thy mortal foe that ever put spear in the rest. – Sir Thomas Malory, -Le Morte d'Artur

In medieval chivalry, knights upheld ideals that included not only valor and prowess in battle but also a refined understanding of meekness. Unlike our modern perception of meekness as weakness, knights practiced a disciplined restraint in the face of conflict, guided by principles of honor, justice, and mercy.

The virtue of meekness was evident in their ability to exercise strength with temperance, choosing diplomacy and peace whenever possible while reserving force for just causes. Their embodiment of meekness was part of their understanding of the Christian ideal which reflected a nuanced balance of power and humility, shaping their reputation as guardians of both physical and moral integrity in their communities.

C.S. Lewis understood the value of meekness. He

saw that it placed a double demand on human nature: one cannot be meek if one is incapable of using force but, likewise, the man of strength cannot be meek unless he is restrained. Because of this, the virtue of meekness demands strength from the weak and humility from the strong.

If we cannot produce Launcelots, humanity falls into two sections—those who can deal in blood and iron but cannot be "meek in hall", and those who are "meek in hall" but useless in battle—for the third class, who are both brutal in peace and cowardly in war, need not here be discussed. When this dissociation of the two halves of Launcelot occurs, history becomes a horribly simple affair. The ancient history of the Near East is like that. Hardy barbarians swarm down from their highlands and obliterate a civilization. Then they become civilized themselves and go soft. Then a new wave of barbarians comes down and obliterates them. Then the cycle begins over again. Modern machinery will not change this cycle; it will only enable the same thing to happen on a larger scale. Indeed, nothing much else can ever happen if the "stern" and the "meek" fall into two mutually exclusive classes. And never forget that this is their natural condition. The man who combines both characters—the knight—is a work not of nature but of art; of that art which has human beings, instead of canvas or marble, for its medium. -C.S. Lewis, The Necessity of Chivalry

Meekness does not use its power for its own defense or selfish purposes. It is not weakness but πραΰς, praus, gentleness. It describes the man whose temper is always under complete control. It means power with restraint.

Meekness does not use its power for its own defense or selfish purposes. It is not weakness but πραΰς, praus, gentleness. It describes the man whose temper is always under complete control. It means power with restraint.

The man of meekness knows when to be angry and when to silence his rage. He patiently bears the wrongs visited upon himself yet is chivalrously ready to spring to the defense of others who are wronged. When he becomes angry, he is aroused by that which maligns God's Name or His work or is harmful to others, not by what is done against himself. And when he does demonstrate righteous anger, it is controlled and carefully directed, not a careless and wild release of emotion that hurts everyone who is near.

Praus is the warhorse, strong yet tame. Gentle is the knight who stands for those who cannot stand for themselves.

> ...The man who is praus is the man who is kindled by indignation at the wrongs and the sufferings of others but is never moved to anger by the wrongs and the insults he himself has to bear.
>
> -William Barclay

[22]

The Deterioration of Faith

When I began this article, I intended to share the story of my conversion. However, as I started writing, I found myself drawn to the very things that had caused me to abandon the faith in the first place. I found there may be more value in discussing what pushed me away—those same things that affect so many young men today. By sharing the reasons behind my spiritual abdication, I hope to provide an understanding of what drives men like myself to step away from Christianity and what brings them back.

The first crack in my faith was the lack of intellectual rigor. The faith tradition in which I was raised was ill-prepared to handle the questions posed by the modern world. I first noticed these intellectual deficiencies around the age of nine. My Sunday school teacher asked the class, "When you get to heaven, who do you want to meet?" Being a history-obsessed kid, I quickly responded with my hero: "Julius Caesar." She immediately reminded me that Caesar wasn't a Christian. I pointed out that Caesar had lived before Christ, so he couldn't deny Him, and therefore was not a Christian. She remained adamant that Caesar was not in heaven, and this led to an argument about the fate of those who lived and died without knowledge of Christ.

I asked about the uncontacted tribes in the Amazon (an interest of mine sparked by my grandmother's National Geographic collection). My Sunday school teacher had no answer. From that point on, the questions began to pile up, but answers rarely followed. Rather than encouraging curiosity, my questions seemed unwelcome. By the time I reached my twenties, I was fully engaged with the New Atheist movement, reading Dawkins and Harris. The God Delusion eventually fell into my orbit, and it gave me the answers I had been seeking for years. Armed with a sense of intellectual superiority, I questioned everything—and no preacher I encountered could stand up to my inquiries. I felt that the intellectual foundation of Christianity had crumbled beneath rationalism.

The second blow to my faith was the lack of spiritual seriousness. Growing up, I never felt a sense of the sacred. Contemporary worship felt more like a concert than an act of reverence. How were worship music and smoke machines appropriate for honoring the Creator of the Universe? Instead of deep religious conviction, what I encountered felt more like self-help, feel-good "prosperity spirituality." Even in the more traditional worship service, I felt a lack of awe and wonder.

Perhaps the most damaging factor was the lack of masculine influence in my spiritual life. Everywhere I looked, the world of religion seemed dominated by women. I saw my mother pray regularly and listened to my grandmother's quote scripture. But I rarely saw men pray outside of grace before meals. The preachers I encountered were often overweight and spoke in that unsettling televangelist cadence. I don't know that I ever saw a choir director I believed was straight, and the youth pastors were often the kind of kids I had bullied in high school.

I struggled to find masculine role models within the church. Even the Christian heroes of my youth—though they were men of faith—didn't seem to put it at the forefront of their lives. Their faith was secondary, or nonexistent. I desired examples of strong, masculine men who placed their beliefs at the center of their lives, but they were nowhere to be found. Without these role models, I was left feeling spiritually unmoored, as if the faith was something that men took part in peripherally, rather than as a core part of their identity, something their wives made them do.

This is not meant to be "a case for Catholicism." However, every rationale I had for leaving the faith was dismantled by Catholic theology. Its intellectual tradition—whether you agree with it or not—stands second to none and there I found answers I had long been seeking. Every question the New Atheists posed as if it elevated them above religious superstition was dismantled in the writings of Aquinas and Augustine, and there was no answer the catechism could not provide.

Catholicism gave me the intellectual rigor I had longed for, but it also offered something deeper: a sense of the sacred. The sacrifice of the Mass, the sacraments, the dogma, it provided a level of spiritual gravity that had long been missing in my life. These traditions were infused into my daily life, forcing me to engage with my faith at every moment. And for once I finally saw masculine men whose faith was front and center—kings, knights, saints. Men of action and deep conviction.

For me, Catholicism answered both the intellectual and spiritual questions that had plagued me for years. It provided the sense of awe and reverence I had been missing, and it reintroduced me to a Christianity where men played a prominent and respectable role. Again, this is not meant to lead anyone toward Catholicism, but rather to explain what tore me away from faith and what ultimately brought me back.

When my Protestant brothers and sisters read this, I hope it sheds light on why so many young men are drawn to Catholicism and Orthodoxy. It's not just about doctrinal differences but about finding a faith tradition that offers intellectual depth, spiritual seriousness, and strong male role models. Many young men today are seeking something more—something that offers both conviction and strength in the face of modernity.

Of course, many within Protestantism find deep meaning in their faith, and for them, contemporary worship styles or a lack of historical tradition may not pose the same challenges. However, for me, the search for something more, something intellectually and spiritually robust led me elsewhere. I hope that by understanding what led me astray—and ultimately brought me back—others might find ways to strengthen their faith tradition, something to help young men hold tight to Christ.

[23]

The Rise of Vitalism and the Failure of ConInc Masculinity

The bull does not suffer the fly on his horns

– Latin Maxim

Over the last few years, I've watched Conservative Inc. attempt — and fail — to combat the growing appeal of vitalism. Large numbers of young men continue to gravitate toward figures like Andrew Tate and Bronze Age Pervert (BAP). The reasons for this trend are straightforward: these young men have grown up in a world devoid of strong, masculine influence. A starving man will eat anything.

Their teachers are women, their bosses are women, and increasingly, their political leaders are women. From the moment they step inside a school, masculine tendencies are suppressed, if not outright condemned. Depending on their home environment, this emasculation may begin even earlier. It's no wonder that lacking genuine masculine guidance; they seek refuge in figures who promise to restore the very essence of manhood that society stifles.

Andrew Tate and Bronze Age Pervert appeal to this hunger. They tell young men to embrace their masculinity, to rise above the feminized world they've inherited, and to fight back. They speak directly to the core frustrations of these young men in a language of confidence, aggression, and defiance.

Conservative Inc.'s response, by contrast, has been limp-wristed at best. Early attempts to compete with the vitalist aesthetic resulted in superficial displays — podcast studios decked out in mahogany, cigars clamped between bearded jaws, all wrapped in faux-masculine posturing. While this illusion of ruggedness had some impact, it was never enough.

There are many expressions of masculinity. Not every man is destined to be Rambo. Some are builders, some are thinkers, and some are spiritual guides. While I believe all men should cultivate physical strength, it's not every man's calling to be a warrior. However, a certain subset of young men is drawn to raw, aggressive, hyper-masculine ideals.

For these young men, vitalism — with its unapologetically brash and take-no-prisoners ethos — is extremely seductive. They admire the loud, aggressive energy that refuses to bend. Conservative

Inc. fails to understand these men. Their tone-deaf attempts to reach them either fall on deaf ears or provoke ridicule.

Figures like Matt Walsh and Joel Berry respond by wagging fingers and issuing stern admonishments. They scold these men as hedonistic, sinful, or degenerate. And to what end? The vitalist young man, already conditioned to resent moralistic lecturing, sees Walsh and Berry as no different from the schoolmarms and authority figures who've belittled his masculinity since childhood.

This is what Walsh and Berry fail to grasp: they are perceived as weak by the vitalist young man. At best, they resemble the sitcom dad — docile, domesticated, and content to live a quiet life in the suburbs. The truth of their character doesn't matter. What matters is perception. The vitalist young man seeks adventure, risk, and conquest. He craves strength and boldness, and as a result, he is unwilling — even unable — to take advice from anyone he views as weak.

Again, this isn't to say Walsh and Berry are weak. Perhaps they aren't. But to this specific type of young man, they will always be seen that way.

Not every young man looks to Andrew Tate as a role model, but those who do are drawn to him because he projects strength. To reach these men, you must appear strong. You cannot turn their gaze from a Bugatti by offering them a minivan.

Instead of dismissing these men, we should

recognize the underlying desires driving them. A generation of young men yearns for strength, risk, and purpose. They want mentors who can teach them to harness their masculine energy, not suppress it. Conservative Inc. is staffed by company men, and company men are not vitalist men. What we need are men who, like Teddy Roosevelt, combined moral discipline with rugged action.

If you want to turn men away from Tate or BAP, offer them a vision of manhood that is unapologetically strong and rightly ordered — one that inspires men to channel their raw power toward building, defending, and leading with purpose. Only then can we turn the tide and win back the allegiance of these disillusioned men.

Without this shift, the next generation will be left to learn from those who exploit their frustrations, rather than guide them toward fulfillment.

Again, you cannot sell a minivan to a man looking for a Bugatti

[24]

The Forgotten Tradition of Christian Combat

The knights are dust,
And their good swords are rust,
Their souls are with the saints, we trust
-The History of the Knights Templars

The relationship between Christianity and violence is a thread I've been unraveling for some time. It's a complex and often misunderstood topic, particularly in today's world. When we survey the Christian landscape, it becomes apparent that violence, especially in defense of the faith, is now widely considered unchristian. The very notion of using force to confront evil has become so unpopular that we tolerate actions and behaviors that would have been inconceivable to Christians of the past. Consider, for example, the statue of Satan standing in the Iowa State Capitol—an act that would have been unthinkable to a Christian just a hundred years ago. Yet modern Christians are often told that opposing such things would be intolerant and, worse, unchristian.

But how did we get here? How did Christians lose their teeth?

Today, interpretations of "love thy neighbor" abound, with countless sermons preaching a form of suicidal pacifism, all in the name of nonviolence and tolerance.

Yet, a striking paradox emerges. The same Bible verses now used to advocate tolerance were once the rallying cries of Christendom's fiercest warriors—men who shared more in common with monks than with everyday Christians. These were deeply devout men, whose faith would likely put even the most earnest modern believers to shame.

Understanding how these warriors of faith perceived the relationship between Christianity and violence is not only intriguing but vital. For many, myself included, one of the most significant barriers to engaging with today's Church is its overly passive, often feminized nature. What role is there for a man, for a husband and father, in a Church that elevates tolerance to the highest virtue?

It wasn't always this way. Medieval Christian warriors, especially members of holy orders like the Knights Templar and the Hospitallers, held a profoundly different view of how faith and violence could coexist. Their mission was crystal clear: to defend the faith with sword in hand, protecting Christendom. They carried out their duty with full conviction that they were fulfilling God's will.

In the medieval period, military religious orders such as the Knights Templar and the Knights Hospitaller emerged as defenders of Christian lands and protectors of pilgrims. Sanctioned by the Church, these men committed their lives to prayer, contemplation, and the defense of the faith. For them, violence wasn't merely permitted—it was sanctified. They saw themselves as part of a divine martial tradition.

For these military orders, taking up arms was not just a right but a divine expectation. They believed they were the protectors of the faithful, with their actions rooted in scripture. Nicolaus von Jeroschin, a 14th-century chronicler of the Teutonic Knights, provides insight into their mindset. He refers to Old Testament figures like Abraham, who led men to rescue his brother Lot from captivity, as divine precedents for their actions.

Jeroschin writes:

> *This praiseworthy order of knights was not only confirmed by the decision of men here on earth, but gracious God in heaven has also confirmed it and praised it in the heavenly kingdom and given many prefigurations of it... We can read in the Old Testament that good Abraham, the great patriarch, chose 318 of his men and rode with them against the heathens to fight for his brother, Lot, whom they had taken prisoner, freed him*

and all those in prison with him from their captivity and defeated the heathens in battle. When he was on his way home from the battle Abraham met Melchizedek, who, I have read, was both king and priest, who gave him bread and wine and encouraged him always to pursue blessings from God on high, whose protection allowed him to defeat his enemy.

From this time the faithful began to enter into fierce knightley battles against the heathens. It was also at this time that the Holy Ghost revealed how the head of the church should show favour to knights, bless them and receive them into the protection of the church and should also confirm with privileges and deeds their rights to benefit from the use of any of the property good people gave to them as an act of piety. This body of knights is the most pleasing of its kind and rightly so, because it has sworn itself to avenge God's torments and His crucifixion and to fight for the Holy Land, which rightfully belonged to Christians but had been seized by the heathens..[25]

From these biblical accounts, Jeroschin draws a clear line between medieval knights and Old Testament warriors, suggesting that God had always called upon certain men to protect the faithful. In much the same way that Abraham fought for his people, these Christian knights believed they were divinely appointed to defend the Church and fight its enemies.

As Jeroschin notes:

St. John saw the church militant coming down from heaven like the New Jerusalem, and among other heavenly hordes

> *were the angels' potestates, who fight to drive off the devil's power. Potestates means the powerful ones, and this proves to us that the church is meant to have this knighthood, which protects it and by its mighty power drives off the forces of unbelief and all visible dangers, just as the potestates exerted themselves to protect Christianity from invisible threats, It is clear that by engaging in warfare the knights of the Teutonic Order drive danger away from Christendom.David was a king of whom God approved, whom He himself chose for his people's kingdom. He was also a great prophet and had foreknowledge of future events. For this reason he knew in advance of this body of knights and wanted to prefigure them as they were to be. He chose two tribes from among his people, one called the Cherethites and the other the Pelethites, and gave them the task of protecting him from all danger, according to the meaning of their names: 'Cherethite' means much the same as 'destroyer'; 'Pelethite' means 'wonderful Rescuer.*[26]

This tradition found its roots in stories like those of King David's Cherethites and Pelethites, symbolic protectors of the king. These biblical warriors were precursors to the holy knights, who were seen as defenders of Christ, the true head of the Church. Knights were celebrated not only for their willingness to die in battle but also for their care for the sick and poor, defending Christian lands from both physical and spiritual threats.

Unlike today, where violence is seen as inherently unchristian, these holy warriors were driven by a belief that they were executing divine justice. Their motto, Non nobis Domine, non nobis, sed nomini tuo da gloriam—"Not unto us, O Lord, not unto us, but to Your name give glory"—was a clear statement that their actions, even in battle, were dedicated to the glory of God, not personal gain.

> *They are true knights and elect warriors who risk death for the honour of God. For the sake of their Father's land they destroy and eradicate the enemies of the faith with a strong arm. In the abundance of their love the good knights receive guests, pilgrims and the poor. They also take pity on the sick, lying in all manner of distress in hospitals, whom they tend generously, humbly and ardently in the course of their duty.*[27]

These knights were not just warriors; they were symbolic protectors, whose role was to shield the king. The knights of Christendom were similarly tasked with protecting Christian lands from physical and spiritual threats, seeing themselves as defenders of Christ, the true head of the Church.

Throughout Christian history, the tension between peace and violence has been navigated through doctrines such as Just War theory. First articulated by St. Augustine and later expanded by St. Thomas Aquinas, this theory laid down clear guidelines for when and how war could be morally justified.[28]

The knights of the medieval Church were well aware of these teachings. They didn't view their position as warriors as a blank check for violence. Instead, they clung to strict principles, only taking up arms when they believed it was necessary and righteous. St. Bernard of Clairvaux, in In Praise of the New Knighthood, warns against the dangers of secular warfare. He stresses that fighting with sinful motives—such as the desire for conquest or revenge—would damn the soul, even in victory. For Bernard, the morality of warfare wasn't determined by the outcome but by the purity of the heart and the righteousness of the cause.

> *As often as thou who wagest a secular warfare marchest forth to battle, it is greatly to be feared lest when thou slayest thine enemy in the body, he should destroy thee in the spirit, or lest peradventure thou shouldst be at once slain by him both in body and soul. From the disposition of the heart, indeed, not by the event of the fight, is to be estimated either the jeopardy or the victory of the Christian. If, fighting with the desire of killing another, thou shouldest chance to get killed thyself, thou diest a man-slayer; if, on the other hand, thou prevailest, and through a desire of conquest or revenge killest a man, thou livest a man-slayer.... O unfortunate victory, when in overcoming thine adversary thou fallest into sin, and anger or pride having the mastery over thee, in vain thou gloriest over the vanquished.*[29]

St. Bernard's words make it clear that the morality of war lies not in winning or losing, but in the condition of the soul and the righteousness of the motives. Fighting with desires for conquest or revenge would corrupt the soul, turning even a physical victory into a spiritual defeat.

> *What, therefore, is the fruit of this secular, I will not say 'militia,' but 'malitia,' if the slayer committeth a deadly sin, and the slain perisheth eternally? Verily, to use the words of the apostle, he that ploweth should plow in hope, and he that thresheth should be partaker of his hope. Whence, therefore, O*

soldiers, cometh this so stupendous error? What insufferable madness is this—to wage war with so great cost and labour, but with no pay except either death or crime?[30]

By contrast, knights of the Holy Orders fought not for personal gain but for the glory of God. As St. Bernard emphasizes, the soldiers of Christ fight the battles of their Lord, unafraid of sin from the slaughter of enemies or the danger of their own death. In this framework, death in service to Christ was not a crime but a pathway to glory. This allowed the knights to engage in battle with a clear conscience, confident they were fulfilling divine justice.

However, Bernard also underscores that violence was to be a last resort, used only when absolutely necessary. He writes:

I do not mean to say that the pagans are to be slaughtered when there is any other way to prevent them from harassing and persecuting the faithful, but only that it now seems better to destroy them than that the rod of sinners be lifted over the lot of the just, and the righteous perhaps put forth their hands unto iniquity.[31]

He continues...

What then? If it is never permissible for a Christian to strike with the sword, why did the Savior's precursor bid the soldiers to be content with their pay, and not rather forbid them to follow this calling? But if it is permitted to all those so destined by God, as is indeed the case provided they have not embraced a higher calling, to whom, I ask, may it be allowed

> *more rightly than to those whose hands and hearts hold for us Sion, the city of our strength?*[32]

Thus, even within the framework of just war, there remained a profound caution against the irresponsible use of violence.

What set the Holy Orders apart from secular knights was not just their motivations, but also their strict discipline, both in battle and in daily life. Their rules were steeped in Christian virtue. Unlike the secular warriors of the time, knights of the Holy Orders were expected to shun worldly desires and focus solely on their mission.

> *Before battle, these knights fortified themselves with faith rather than ornamentation. They adorned themselves with armor and steel, not gold, seeking to inspire fear in their enemies rather than admiration for their wealth. Their conduct was dictated by a higher calling, aiming to terrify their foes through their strength, not their appearance.*

> *...on the approach of battle they fortify themselves with faith within, and with steel without, and not with gold, so that, armed and not adorned, they may strike terror into the enemy, rather than awaken his lust of plunder. They strive earnestly to possess strong and swift horses, but not garnished with ornaments or decked with trappings, thinking of battle and of victory, and not of pomp and show, and studying to inspire fear rather than admiration.*[33]

Outside of battle, the knights devoted themselves to caring for the sick, tending to the wounded, and living a life of quiet contemplation and religious devotion. The Rule of the Templars, for instance, emphasized humility and simplicity. Knights were forbidden from owning private wealth, and any splendor they received had to be muted to avoid fostering pride. Their mission was to serve God, not to seek personal glory.[34]

If a brother acquired any money, it was tied around his neck and he was led naked through the house with another brother beating him severely.[35]

Even contact with women was strictly limited.

> *LASTLY. We hold it dangerous to all religion to gaze too much on the countenance of women; and therefore no brother shall presume to kiss neither widow, nor virgin, nor mother, nor sister, nor aunt, nor any other woman. Let the knighthood of Christ shun feminine kisses, through which men have very often been drawn into danger, so that each, with a pure conscience and secure life, may be able to walk everlastingly in the sight of God.*[36]

> *The Laws of the Teutonic Knights are more succinct: it is a fault when a brother on a journey knowingly, and secretly or openly, consorts with bad women.*[37]

Similarly, the Statutes of the Teutonic Knights strictly regulated battlefield conduct. Cowardice in battle or fleeing from the Christian army was seen as the gravest sin, one that could lead to expulsion from the Order. The knights understood that their duty was to fight with both courage and integrity, knowing that their actions on the battlefield reflected their commitment to Christ.

> *If a brother in cowardice flees from the standard or from the army," or "goes over from the Christians to the heathen," he was committing the most serious sin, for which was no pardon or redress and he is lost the Order forever.*[38]

When the Knight of the holy order met the enemy he had only one choice summarized in the words of Hartman von Aue.

Nu zinzent, ritter,
dein leben und such den geist
durch in who in da hat
gegeben liebe under gut
Das er da wol gevert
Daz giltet beidiu teil
Der werlte lop er sele heil[39]

Now pay interest, knight,
your life and also your spirit
Through in who has given
love and good spirit
His belief in this gives him
A chance of seeing glory
in both parts of the world
and the salvation of the soul[40]

So, how did we go from knights of the cross to a

Church that preaches near-total nonviolence? Several key factors contributed to this shift. One major influence was the Protestant Reformation, which rejected many of the medieval Church's teachings, including those surrounding holy warfare. The Enlightenment further reshaped Christian thought, with its emphasis on human reason, individual rights, and a growing distaste for religiousness.

The trauma of the world wars also played a significant role, as did the rise of globalism. In a pluralistic world that values tolerance and peace, the idea of using violence to defend the faith has become increasingly unpopular. Modern Christianity, particularly in the West, has moved away from the martial mindset of the medieval Church, embracing pacifism and tolerance as its highest virtue.

While the modern Church has largely embraced pacifism and tolerance, history shows that the relationship between Christianity and violence is far more nuanced. Medieval Christians, particularly the holy orders, saw a place for righteous violence in defense of the faith. They did not glorify violence for its own sake, but they understood it as sometimes necessary to protect what was sacred.

Perhaps modern Christians can find wisdom in this history. While nonviolence and tolerance are indeed virtues, so too are strength, courage, and the willingness to defend what is holy. The challenge lies in rediscovering the balance between these ideals, understanding that there is room in the Christian tradition for both the monk and the warrior, that often they are one and the same.

[25]

The Twilight of Warriors

In ancient societies, the peak of the hierarchy was occupied by the caste of warrior aristocracy, whereas today, in the pacifist-humanitarian utopias (especially in the Anglo-Saxon ones), attempts are made to portray the warrior as some kind of anachronism, and as a dangerous and harmful entity that one day will be conveniently disposed of in the name of progress.

-Julius Evola, Meditations on the Peaks.

Does the warrior still exist? The answer is far more complicated than it might seem. While many might immediately point to modern military members, such as infantry or Special Forces operators, the true essence of a warrior requires deeper examination. Having engaged in extensive discussions on this topic, I've found that the resistance, especially from fellow veterans, arises from a fundamental misunderstanding. This debate is not merely about definitions; it reflects a deeper conflict between a materialist perspective and a metaphysical interpretation of what it means to be a warrior.

In ancient societies, the warrior was more than a warfighter, he was a crucial part of the aristocracy and set at the top of the social hierarchy—the warrior exemplified the values of honor, bravery, and spiritual discipline, he was the defender of culture. Today, however, modern societies tend to dismiss the cultural and social aspects of the warrior.

> *The warrior becomes interchangeable with the professional soldier. This shift in perception reflects a broader societal move towards egalitarianism and technological efficiency in warfare, overlooking the metaphysical and cultural significance that warriors once held. "The warrior caste occupied a specific position in this hierarchy, responsible for upholding and defending the social order and values of the society.*
>
> *-Julius Evola*[41]

The warrior extends beyond the battlefield, he was an essential part of the warrior caste. Traditional societies were hierarchically structured, with a clear division of roles and duties. A true warrior was not merely a fighter but rather a person with a profound spiritual dimension. While we can easily compare the martial prowess of a Green Beret to that of a medieval knight—both masters of their craft, honing their skills to become proficient in combat—there is a notable absence of a spiritual dimension in the Green Beret (or any other modern military unit). While an individual Green Beret may have personal faith or piety, his spirituality remains independent of his role as a warrior. Julius Evola underscored the significance of the warrior's inner life, highlighting dedication to discipline and adherence to higher, transcendent principles. He emphasized that "the warrior's actions reflected a metaphysical struggle, symbolizing a battle against chaos and materialism."[42]

> *Traditional warrior values contrast sharply with the decadence and mediocrity of modern, egalitarian societies and militaries. – Julius Evola*

The warrior caste of old embodied aristocratic and heroic values such as honor, bravery, loyalty, and duty, which permeated every aspect of their lives. These values shaped their world, influencing their daily routines, their habits, and their overall lifestyle. Knights adhered strictly to the chivalric code; the Knights Templar, known for their piety and dedication, adhered to stringent rules. They were forbidden from owning property or receiving private correspondence, prohibited from marrying or becoming betrothed outside their order, and could not take vows in any other order. Additionally, they were required to remain debt-free and free from any physical infirmities.[43]

For the Samurai, the Bushido code demanded an equally high level of dedication. Practices such as Kiri-sute gomen permitted a Samurai to strike down any member of a lower class who dishonored them.

Seppuku, or ritual suicide, offered a path to die honorably or to restore lost honor.[44]

The warrior caste was not just a military force but also a guiding and stabilizing influence on society. Warriors were seen as custodians of order and guardians of the sacred traditions and principles that underpin a well-functioning society. The warrior caste was the bedrock of their civilizations, representing the highest values of their societies.

There is nothing offered by modern militaries that is analogous to the cultural and social impact of chivalry or bushido. Modern militaries often emphasize "Core Values" such as honor, courage, and commitment. However, these values today are often seen as a crude imitation of their historical counterparts. Unlike warriors of the past, modern soldiers are not willing to commit Seppuku to restore honor, nor do they typically shun earthly possessions or lead celibate lives. Likewise, the values of the military have little to no bearing on the border culture and are often seen (even in their diluted form) as archaic.

Indeed, warriors of the past did not always adhere strictly to the codes they lived by. Knights sometimes squabbled over petty disagreements or retreated from the battlefield, and Samurai were known to abuse their authority. However, these instances do not diminish the significance of the codes they upheld. More often than not, these codes were societal norms that guided their conduct and defined their roles and cannot be dismissed simply because some individuals failed to uphold them consistently.

Ernst Jünger recognized the impact of technology on the battlefield, acknowledging that it had rendered traditional chivalric and heroic concepts of the warrior unsustainable. He understood that skill and courage no longer guaranteed glory or survival when enormous military machines mercilessly devoured the human "matériel" fed into them, reducing men to "a kind of charcoal, which is hurled under the glowing cauldron of war so as to keep the work going."[45]

In The Glass Bees, Jünger reflects on the final charge of the cavalry in the face of this new industrialized war:

> *The old Centaurs were overpowered by the new Titan. I had seen my own conqueror at close hand when I lay bleeding on the grass. He had unhorsed me – a sickly fellow, a pimply lad from the suburbs, some cutler from Sheffield or weaver from Manchester. He cowered behind his rubble heap, one eye shut, the other aiming at me across the machine gun, which did the damage. In a pattern of red and gray, he wove an evil cloth. This was the new Polyphemus or, rather, one of his lowest messenger boys with a wire mask before his one-eyed face. This was how the present masters looked. The beauty of the forests was past. – Ernst Jünger*

The transition from the valorous individual combat of warriors to the mechanized, impersonal warfare of modern soldiers highlights a fundamental shift. The essence of the warrior, with his spiritual and metaphysical dimensions, has no place in the context of modern, technologically advanced warfare.

Words had lost their meaning; even war was no longer war. Monteron would tum in his grave if he could hear what they called war nowadays. – Ernst Jünger

The transition from warriors to large-scale professional armies unfolded gradually over time. Advances in military technology progressively increased the distance between combatants, rendering individual military prowess less decisive. Many historians cite the Battle of Crécy, where the English longbow proved dominant, as marking the decline of the European Knight. The introduction of firearms further widened this gap and ultimately spelled the end for traditional knights. Concurrent advancements in agriculture and manufacturing enabled the fielding of large armies equipped with inexpensive rifles and trained quickly. Warfare evolved into a disciplined science, emphasizing tactics, maneuverability, and technological proficiency, leaving little room for the romanticized image of the warrior. A poignant illustration of this transformation is the Battle of Shimoyama, where 500 Samurai confronted 30,000 Japanese soldiers.

Despite their training and tradition, all 500 Samurai perished by the battle's end, illustrating the inexorable shift from individual heroism towards modern military tactics and technologies. Despite this shift, warrior traits persist.[46]

The essence of the warrior is not purely in the temporal realm but in the metaphysical, manifesting in the courage and actions of modern soldiers.6 The warrior caste as a societal structure is gone and will remain so unless we return to a more primitive state or technological advancement allows for the return of hand-to-hand combat. Regardless, the spirit of the warrior caste remains, and their influence can still be seen in WWI fighter pilots, and the special forces operators of today, but as we move further away from a time when the warrior truly existed, that residue becomes less and less.

The debate between warriors and soldiers is not just about battlefield outcomes but about the values and ideals that societies uphold. The concept of the warrior should not be seen purely in material terms. It is metaphysical and manifests in the temporal realm. The warrior's spirit and ethos transcend time and technology, manifesting in the courage, honor, and loyalty of those who serve, even the soldiers of today. While modern militaries have proven tactically superior in many instances, the warrior's role in upholding cultural, spiritual, and moral values should not be forgotten.

War may indeed be a dirty business, but the myth, honor, and spirit of the warrior should continue to inspire and guide us. The contributions of warriors go beyond combat effectiveness. They embody the highest ideals of their cultures, serving as enduring symbols of bravery, honor, and transcendence. The essence of the warrior, with its spiritual and metaphysical dimensions, reminds us that beyond the practicalities of warfare, there is a deeper struggle for meaning, order, and the preservation of higher values. The warrior spirit, though seemingly anachronistic, continues to inspire and may hold the key to restoring the very foundations of civilization.

[26]

American Foederati

> I say, therefore, that the arms with which a prince defends his state are either his own, or they are mercenaries, auxiliaries, or mixed. Mercenaries and auxiliaries are useless and dangerous; and if one holds his state based on these arms, he will stand neither firm nor safe; for they are disunited, ambitious, and without discipline, unfaithful, valiant before friends, cowardly before enemies; they have neither the fear of God nor fidelity to men, and destruction is deferred only so long as the attack is; for in peace one is robbed by them, and in war by the enemy. – Niccolò Machiavelli

There has been significant discussion surrounding the United States Military's struggle to meet recruitment goals in recent times. In 2022, the U.S. Army fell short of its recruiting target by approximately 15,000 soldiers, marking a 25% deficit.[47] Concurrently, both the Navy and Air Force failed to meet their recruitment goals by 10%. Despite attempts to address the recruitment crisis by lowering standards and increasing benefits, 2024 is projected to be the military's worst recruiting year since 1945.

The latest plan to increase military recruitment, the Courage to Serve Act is a bipartisan bill aimed at boosting military readiness by offering illegal immigrants an expedited path to citizenship in exchange for military service. If you think it's a bad idea, you're not wrong, just ask our historical doppelganger, Rome.

During the later stages of her existence Rome, much like the United States, struggled to motivate her citizens to join the military. The difficulty in recruiting Roman citizens stemmed from years of poor governance and exploitation. Economic challenges, heavy taxation, social and political instability eroded any sense of civic duty and loyalty among Roman citizens.

Declining agricultural production and hyperinflation sent the economy into decline which played a pivotal role in shaping the reluctance of Roman citizens to engage in military service. Widespread poverty gripped the population, discouraging individuals from pursuing a career in the military, which seemed less appealing compared to potential economic opportunities in alternative fields.

To cope with economic challenges and fund military campaigns, the Roman government imposed heavy taxes on the population, which further exacerbated the economic difficulties faced by her citizens. Because the taxation policies disproportionately affected the lower and middle classes, which traditionally provided a significant portion of the Roman military recruitment. This only added to the economic burden that stifled the population, and as a result the willingness and ability of individuals from these classes to enlist in the military faltered.

To make matters worse Rome began to cut what few incentives remained for military service. The traditional practice of distributing land to retired soldiers, known as the ager publicus, was slowly removed. The erosion of this long-standing reward system weakened the allure of military service, as individuals were no longer guaranteed land for their dedication and sacrifice. The removal of ager publicus in addition to the political instability and frequent leadership changes during the later periods of the Roman Empire created a sense of disillusionment among citizens, that not only saw Romans avoid military service but the abdication of civic duty more broadly.

Despite Rome's struggles to recruit enough soldiers from its citizenry, the persistent external threats and invasions by various barbarian groups necessitated a substantial military force. The demand for such a force consistently outstripped the number of Romans willing to enlist voluntarily. The challenging geopolitical landscape and frequent incursions by barbarian groups placed an enduring strain on Rome that required robust military presence, placing further strain on the tension between the demand for defense and the supply of willing volunteers.

To address the shortage, the Roman army turned to Foederati (non-Roman soldiers and mercenaries) to bolster the legions. As the Roman military became increasingly dependent on the Foederati system, they began offering various incentives—often at the expense of Roman citizens—in exchange for military service. One primary incentive was the allocation of land within the borders of the Roman Empire, enabling soldiers to farm and establish communities. Non-Roman soldiers were frequently granted special legal status within the Empire, exempting them from certain taxes and legal obligations that applied to Roman citizens.

The Foederati system emerged as a response to Rome's inability to mobilize its citizens for the Empire. However, the heightened reliance on mercenaries altered the face of the Roman military. Once the most powerful Romanizing force globally, the army rapidly took on the identity of its new members. German terminology and customs, such as the barritus, an old German battle cry, became widespread. Contemporary writings indicate that the German term "barbarus" (barbarian) and the Latin "miles" (soldier) began to be used interchangeably. This compositional shift further distanced Roman citizens from military institutions, as they felt less connected to an army that was becoming less Roman. The reliance on mercenaries created a negative feedback loop: the more Rome depended on mercenaries, the more it discouraged citizens from joining, and the fewer citizens joined, the more Rome relied on mercenaries.

The introduction of foreign troops was intended to address Rome's immediate military and economic challenges; however, in reality, it introduced several long-term issues that played a substantial role in the decline of the Western Roman Empire.

As the Foederati system grew, it increased the number of ethnic and cultural groups within Roman society, making it difficult to maintain a cohesive identity and unity. This led to increased internal divisions that undermined the empire's stability. The distribution of land to Foederati also intensified strain on the local Roman population, sparking resource competition and disputes over land ownership. The economic struggles that Rome was already facing were aggravated under the added weight of supporting the expansive military structure, and the Foederati.

While the Foederati were undeniably exceptional warriors, their allegiance to the empire waned over time. Armed with knowledge of Roman military tactics, a significant number of the Foederati ultimately turned against Rome.

By the late 4th century, several Germanic

Foederati, including Vandals, Alans, and Suebi, turned against the Roman Empire. In 378 AD, the Visigoths, led by Fritigern, revolted due to mistreatment and food shortages, resulting in a significant defeat for the Romans and the death of the Eastern Roman Emperor Valens. Subsequently, in 410 AD, Alaric, leader of the Visigoths and a former member of the Roman army, besieged and successfully sacked Rome. The culmination of these events occurred in 455 AD when the Vandals, under the leadership of Genseric, once again sacked the city of Rome.

These events dealt severe blows to the prestige and stability of the Western Roman Empire, significantly contributing to its decline. While the Foederati system initially addressed immediate needs, it ultimately led to internal strife, weakened the core of the Roman military, and facilitated external invasions.

Rome's experience is not unique; numerous empires throughout history have grappled with the pitfalls of relying on mercenaries or foreign troops. In the First Punic War (264–241 BC), Carthage encountered challenges in maintaining and compensating its mercenary forces, ultimately contributing to its defeat at the hands of Rome. The Byzantine Empire, particularly during later periods, extensively employed foreign mercenaries, including the Varangians and troops from various regions. While effective in certain instances, the loyalty of mercenaries proved unpredictable, resulting in many instances of betrayal.

The Ottoman Empire, at different points in its history, similarly turned to mercenaries and soldiers from diverse ethnic and religious backgrounds. The Janissaries, an elite Ottoman infantry composed of Christian slaves converted to Islam, played a pivotal role in the empire's military. However, concerns about their loyalty arose over time, prompting reforms and ultimately leading to their dissolution in the early 19th century.

> *...there is no loyalty or inducement to keep them on the field apart from the little they are paid . . . [which] is not enough to make them want to die for you.*
> – *Niccolo Machiavelli*[48]

> The most famous critic of mercenary armies Niccolò Machiavelli saw the danger firsthand. During the Renaissance, several Italian city-states, such as Florence and Venice, relied on mercenary companies, known as condottieri, for their military needs. The shifting loyalties of these mercenary captains often led to complex and unpredictable political dynamics. It was this experience that led him to write extensively on the dangers of the reliance on mercenaries. He strongly advises rulers to avoid the use of mercenaries, since they prioritize their own wellbeing over the interests of the prince. According to Machiavelli, "ruin is the inevitable result of a prince's continued dependence on mercenaries."

History is clear on the subject of mercenary armies;

they are neither loyal nor reliable. Despite this the U.S. seems determined to try and buy its way back to military prominence. While the similarities between Rome and America are hard to ignore, one difference stands out: Rome had something to offer, something valuable enough to make the Foederati temporarily functional. The U.S. as far as I can tell does not. So, the question arises: What benefit does citizenship in the U.S. confer that illegal immigrants do not already possess? If anything, one could argue that citizenship is a downgrade with its added tax burden and legal obligations. With little to offer it seems more likely that there will be no Foederati system in America. After all, who would buy a cow they can milk for free?

[27]

The Cosmocentric Family and the Fate of Empires

Can anything be better for a man than to be heir to himself?- Heliogabalus

John Hubbard's *The Fate of Empires* published in 1913 is a short 130-page dissertation that asks one simple question, "Can there be a permanent society or are they all doomed to decline?"[49] Hubbard argues that human behavior is shaped by the dynamic interplay between instinct and reason: instinct drives individuals to prioritize the welfare of the race (ethnos) through ruthless self-sacrifice, and reason guides societal actions toward competition with contemporaries.

This inherent conflict between the individual and the collective creates an antagonistic relationship within each domain. The resolution, according to

Hubbard, “cannot be achieved by either instinct or reason alone.” Reason advocates for the elimination of competition, risking a descent into the pitfalls of socialism, while instinct maintains a low developmental trajectory by sacrificing individual growth for the sake of the race.

Hubbard suggests finding a new suprarational foundation in the religious motive, elevating both propagation and competition. This religious motive transforms the individual into a member of a family with a vested interest in the past and future of the race, aligning personal and societal goals.

The religious motive provides a framework for anchoring our actions in a broader temporal context, attributing the significance of life to its connection with the infinite and the universe. As described by Hubbard, this motive can take either a geocentric or cosmocentric form, distinguished primarily by their temporal orientations. While the geocentric perspective, exemplified by Stoic philosophy, concentrates on the present moment, the cosmocentric outlook, exemplified by Christianity, transcends human conceptions of time. Hubbard asserts that the cosmocentric religious motive is more effective in pursuing racial and societal goals through self-sacrifice than its geocentric counterpart.

According to Hubbard, “Geocentric actions aim for a permanent civilization as an end but fall short, while cosmocentric actions achieve it without explicitly seeking it as an end.” Additionally, the cosmocentric religious motive possesses the capacity to harmonize the rival spirit driven by individual and societal impulses with the reproductive imperative dictated by racial impulses, serving as a mechanism that imparts significance and a cohesive path to both pursuits.

One of the historical examples that Hubbard provides is that of the Roman family. He points to the strength of the family when rooted in a sense of ancestry and offspring, illustrating the critical role of this suprarational sanction. Conversely, Rome's decline coincided with individuals viewing themselves in opposition to the race, leading to the erosion of familial ties and the eventual dissolution of the state in the face of self-indulgent competition.

This self-indulgent competition resulted in the degradation of marriage. Rome knew three forms of marriage, **cofarreatio**, **coemptio**, and **usus**. The first of these confarreatio was a solemn religious form of marriage. The second coemptio was a respected form of civil marriage. The last, a lower form of marriage known as usus was a common law marriage resulting from cohabitation with the "husband," for one year in which the woman passed under the patria potestas of her husband.

By the close of the Republic cofarreatio and coemptio had almost died out and during the height of the Empire usus dominated, but even usus had degraded. It became common for the wife to remain absent from her husband for three nights a year so that she never passed into the power of her husband. The result was that most "marriages," were merely civil contracts dissoluble at pleasure and according to Hubbard, "most Roman men never married at all."

Augustus attempted to reverse the revolt against marriage and revitalize religious fervor. Early in his reign, Augustus enacted his famous reform, the Lex Julia[50] in 18 B.C. It was divided into three parts of which the Lex de maritandis ordinibus[51] was designed to combat the rise in celibacy and sterility through a series of penalties and rewards.

Strict limitations were imposed on the inheritance rights of the unmarried. The transfer of property was contingent on having children, favoring those who were parents. In cases where a husband and wife had offspring, they could mutually inherit each other's possessions. However, if there were no children, only a tenth of the property could be passed on with the remainder going to the state. Furthermore, a widow or widower was granted a two-year period before remarriage became obligatory.

To encourage marriage and family life, incentives were devised. Married men with families were earmarked for promotions, given priority in theater seating, and granted tax relief.

In A.D. 9, Augustus created the Law Pappia Poppaea, which enacted penalties for adultery and complemented Augustus' Lex Iulia de maritandis ordinibus of 18 BC and the Lex Iulia de adulteriis coercendis of 17 BC. Agustin's reforms were taken seriously, as De Montesquieu writes in Considerations on the Causes of the Greatness of the Romans and their Decline,

These laws were not permitted to become a dead letter. Julia herself, the only daughter of Augustus, the widow of Agrippa, the mother of Caius and Lucius Caesar, and the wife of Tiberius, was convicted under the drastic provisions of the Lex de adulteriis, and banished, at the age of thirty-seven, to the barren little island of Pandataria. The sentence was never revoked, and she died in extreme want and misery. Her daughter, of the same name, offended against the same law, and was banished to a small island in the Adriatic.

Furthermore, according to Tacitus,

> *Spies were appointed, who by the Law Pappia Poppaea were encouraged with rewards to watch such as neglected the privileges of marriage, in order that the State, the common parent, might obtain their vacant possessions.*[52]

Nevertheless, the laws failed in their purpose. Tacitus continues...

Not even by this means (Lex Pappia Poppaea) did marriages and the bringing up of children become more in vogue, the advantage of having no children to inherit outweighing the penalty of disobedience.[53]

In A.D. 9, thirty-four years after the enactment of the Lex Julia, Augustus faced significant grievances regarding the high number of unmarried Equites. Recognizing the substantial impact this had, both in itself and as a negative influence on others, the matter became of great consequence to the Emperor. In response, he promptly convened the entire body of the Equestrian Order, directing the assembly to segregate the married and unmarried individuals. According to Echard, Augustus then addressed the unmarried Equestrians...

> *Their lives and Actions have been so peculiar, that he knew not by what name to call them; not by that of Men, for they performed nothing that was manly; nor by that of citizens, for the city might perish notwithstanding their care: nor by that of Romans, for they designed to extirpate the Roman name. Then proceeding to shew his tender care and hearty affection for his people, he further told them. That their course of life was of such pernicious consequence to the glory and grandeur of the Roman Nation, that he could not choose but tell them that all other crimes put together could not equalize theirs: for they were guilty of murder, in not suffering those to be born, which should proceed from them; of impiety, in causing the names and honors of their ancestors to cease; and of sacrilege, in destroying their kind, which proceed from the immortal gods, and human nature, the principal thing consecrated to them therefore, in that respect they dissolved the government, in disobeying its laws; betraying their country, by making it barren and waste; nay and demolished their city, in depriving it of inhabitants, and he was sensible that all this proceeded not from any kind of virtue or abstinence, but from looseness and wantonness which ought never be encouraged in any civil government.*[54]

Fifty years after Augustus' death, Tacitus observed

that "nearly all the Equites and the greater number of the senators betrayed a servile (slave) origin." The decline in marriage and birth rates compelled Rome to rely on a constant influx of aliens, predominantly slaves from the east and German invaders from the north. The manumission of slaves became imperative, as slaves were entitled to a peculium (private savings) for purchasing their freedom. Upon liberation, those of servile birth entered the class of libertines or freedmen, and even in the era of the first Caesar, being born free was sufficient for qualifying as a citizen rather than foreign-born. Citizenship, according to Gibbon, was determined by the mother's condition, "if her freedom could be ascertained, during a single moment, between conception and delivery."

Despite the influx of aliens and servile citizens, Rome's population decline persisted. Hubbard notes, "Reason did not spare the newcomers, and multitudes poured into Italy, only to vanish, like a river flowing into sands."

No leader made as fervent an effort to combat population decline as Augustus. His lifelong endeavor proved unsuccessful, and the Roman world faced the corrosive question of Emperor Heliogabalus, "Can anything be better for a man than to be heir to himself?" Romans concluded that nothing could surpass spending their inheritance on themselves. Twenty-six years after Diocletian's abdication, Constantine shifted the seat of imperial power from the Tiber to the Bosphorus and Lactantius documented the ominous depopulation of Italy and the oppressive taxation burdening the few survivors.

Hubbard's thesis posits that enduring civilizations cannot thrive on instinct or reason alone; their permanence lies in safeguarding racial preservation and tempering pure reason through cosmocentric religious motives and strong family structures. Ad hoc religiousness proves insufficient; history demonstrates that, despite Christians restoring the dignity of marriage during Justinian's time, they could not undo the influence of earlier conditions that rationalized it away.

Hubbard's theory underscores the pivotal roles of religious motives and robust family bonds as essential elements for the enduring vitality of civilizations. Maintaining a balance between instinct and reason becomes crucial to preventing the erosion of societal values. The geocentric religious motive in Rome, primarily serving practical purposes, underscores the detrimental impact of prioritizing individual gratification over familial and societal commitments. Hubbard's insights illuminate the timeless principles that sustain civilizations, emphasizing the imperative integration of reason, instinct, and a transcendent religious foundation for navigating and upholding a civilization.

Religious controversy is the offspring of arrogance and folly;

that true piety is most laudably expressed by silence and submission; that man, ignorant of his own nature, should not presume to scrutinize the nature of his God; and that it is sufficient for us to know, that power and benevolence are the perfect attributes of the Deity.

— Edward Gibbon, The Decline and Fall of the Roman Empire

[28]

The South and Southern Identity

[29]

How does it Profit the South?

As a Southerner, I have always enjoyed the simple joy of driving down the backroads of Alabama. The black top two lanes that cut through the state are beautiful, flanked by old pecan orchards and cattle farms, where rustic tractors sit half visible behind tall grass, like monuments to our agrarian roots. Amongst the hand-painted signs and well-worn service stations that line these roads lies the heart of Alabama.

Yet, the heart of Alabama is changing, and I cannot help but feel a tinge of sorrow as I witness the transformation unfolding before my eyes. The small farms that dotted the landscape have been gradually replaced by sprawling subdivisions, where rows of characterless houses emerge almost overnight. The charming service stations, where old men used to pass the time with stories of old, now yield to the yellow-black glow of Dollar General, emblematic of the creeping homogenization brought about by modernity.

Indeed, the South has seen an industrial renaissance in the past two decades. Lured by the promise of low taxes and a union-free workforce, industries have flocked to our region. Yet, we have always been an agrarian people, our roots deeply intertwined with the land. This seismic shift from agriculture to industry marks a profound change that leaves me with mixed feelings.

As the tech, film, aerospace, and automotive sectors make their way to our warmer climate, the landscape continues to shift. My home state of Alabama has quietly emerged as the automotive capital of the United States, hosting five major manufacturers and one hundred and fifty suppliers, employing thousands of Alabamians. It is the same story across the South. The tech industry in North Carolina now employs close to half a million people, while Texas boasts the title of the largest technology exporter since 2012.

There is no denying that this influx of jobs and tax revenue has brought increased prosperity to the South. Yet, it is bittersweet for me, growing up, the South was often seen as poor, uneducated, and archaic, a land that progress forgot. This perception, in a way, shielded us from external influences. When I graduated high school in 2007 my school still celebrated Robert E. Lee Day and the DMV was closed for Confederate Memorial Day. For the most part, we were left to grow and practice our culture in relative seclusion, hidden away in our hollers and farms. Our poverty and perceived cultural stagnation became a protective cloak, preserving our unique identity.

But, the rapid industrialization and urbanization of the South is a Faustian bargain, threatening the very essence of what makes us who we are. We are already seeing our rich customs, traditions, and values being overshadowed or discarded in the relentless pursuit of profit and conformity. How many statues and headstones now lie in ruins or hidden away in storage lockers because transplants brought forth by the lure of money and employment sought to turn the South into little New England?

The consequences of large corporations dictating our cultural landscape weigh heavily on my mind. In a world driven by mass consumption and fleeting trends, I can't help but worry that the vibrancy and authenticity of our Southern traditions may be reduced to mere commodities, stripped of their true essence and significance. The introduction of conflicting values from diverse backgrounds further compounds these concerns, as it threatens to dilute the very core of our heritage and erode our collective identity.

Moreover, the rapid expansion of urban centers raises valid concerns about the displacement of longstanding communities. Iconic cities like Atlanta and North Carolina's Research Triangle now wield significant influence, overshadowing rural areas and threatening the very fabric that has nurtured our customs and shaped our collective memory for generations.

Reflecting on this situation, I find myself drawn to Christ's words in Mark 8:36, "For what shall it profit a man if he shall gain the whole world, and lose his own soul?" Are we willing our identity for GDP and manicured lawns? Is increased tax revenue worth forced cultural amnesia? I for one do not want a South that is indistinguishable from Ohio or Illinois.

In the face of "Americanization", it is incumbent upon us, as Southerners, to band together and safeguard what is dear to us. We must become active stewards of our culture, tenaciously protecting the traditions that define us. It is crucial to preserve our heritage through grassroots efforts, community involvement, and the passing down of knowledge from one generation to the next. We must teach our sons and daughters to sing "Dixie Land," to hold names like Lee, Jackson, and Davis in reverence because, when money dries up, it will be our children who remain.

Let us celebrate the shared heritage that binds us, cherishing our customs and traditions as treasures to be nurtured and safeguarded. As proud keepers of our cultural richness, we must strive to instill a sense of pride in the next generation. By fostering a collective commitment to our Southern identity, we can create a legacy that stands the test of time and weathers the storms of modernization.

In the midst of rapid change, we must remain steadfast in our dedication to preserving the soul of the American South. Our culture is a tapestry woven from the threads of our ancestors' resilience, our communities' strength, and our vibrant traditions. Our children deserve to experience the backroads, the pecan orchards, cattle farms, and rustic tractors, for they are more than mere scenic beauty – they are symbols of our identity, our roots, and the very essence of who we are as Southerners. With reverence for our past and determination for our future, we can ensure that the heart of Dixie continues to thrive, ever vibrant and deeply cherished, and if all else fails we should remind economic guests, "A Southern man don't need them around anyhow."

[30]

Stranger in a Homeland

I know that everything essential and great originated from the fact that the human being had a homeland and was rooted in tradition.
– Martin Heidegger

A homeland is born from the depth of one's roots, the sacrifices made, and the shared memory of a nation's journey.

My family has been in America since before it was America. My mother's family arrived in the Virginia Colony around 1660. In 1677, where my 9th great-grandfather was executed for his participation in Bacon's Rebellion. By 1760, they had migrated to Georgia, and by 1860, they were living in Natchitoches, before finally settling in Texas after the Civil War.

My father's family has a slightly more interesting story. According to legend, they sided with the King during the English Civil War. When the King was decapitated, they fled Scotland for Württemberg, Germany, until my 7th great-grandfather moved to the colonies around 1750, where he joined the British Army to fight in the French and Indian War.

After the war, he made a home in North Carolina, eventually joining the militia and fighting in the American Revolution. When the war was over, they became one of the first families to settle in Tennessee, where they stayed until moving to Texas in 1901.

For centuries, my family carved a place for themselves in this country. They crossed frontiers and fought in its wars, lending their names to towns, schools, and battlefields. Blood was shed at King's Mountain, Horseshoe Bend, Gettysburg, Chickamauga, Belleau Wood, Guadalcanal, Vietnam, Iraq, and Afghanistan. Each generation left its mark on America's history, creating a deep bond with the land they fought to claim as their home.

They arrived with nothing and built everything. They were heritage Americans.

The term "heritage American" has its share of detractors, but it encapsulates the essence of families like mine, whose stories are fused with every chapter of America's history. They are the families connected to every major event, crisis, and victory this nation has experienced, the families who have seen this country through its darkest hours and its brightest days.

They were pioneers, soldiers, and patriots, pursuing both freedom and fortune. Yet today, we are told that this history—this legacy— the time spent here, the sacrifices made, do not give us a unique claim to the title of "home." We are told that we have no more right to call this land ours than someone who arrived yesterday.

We are told this because we are not ruled by Americans. We are ruled by those whose ancestors did not bleed on her battlefields or toil on her farms. These new stewards, though they drape themselves in our flag, lack a connection to the land, the legacy. Their ancestors weren't at Gettysburg or Concord, they have no connection to the sacrifices made on the beaches of Normandy or in the jungles of Vietnam. They are newcomers with no sense of the nation's past, indifferent to its heroes—Davy Crockett, Daniel Boone, George Washington, Robert E. Lee, Ulysses S. Grant. To them, these figures belong to a dead country. They see themselves as rulers of a new America, and heritage Americans are simply relics—unwelcome reminders of a past they wish to erase.

The America I knew, the one my family helped build, is morphing into something unrecognizable. The walls are the same, the cracks in the floor still tell the stories of those who came before, yet something fundamental has shifted. The place that once felt familiar now feels alien, the air is thick with a sense of displacement. It's disorienting—living as a stranger in your homeland.

But this is still our home, and we must fight, we must live up to the title of Heritage Americans.

> Loving your homeland is just as natural as loving your father or mother – after all, your country nourishes you, protects you, and in many ways makes you who you are. Just as it's a virtue to honor your parents, it's a good and admirable thing to honor the land you call home. -William Bennet

[31]

From Common Origins:The Cultural Fabric of America

> *With equal pleasure I have as often taken notice that Providence has been pleased to give this one connected country to one united people—a people descended from the same ancestors, speaking the same language, professing the same religion, attached to the same principles of government, very similar in their manners and customs, and who, by their joint counsels, arms, and efforts, fighting side by side throughout a long and bloody war, have nobly established general liberty and independence. – John Jay, Federalist No. 2*[55]

America is not a propositional nation. The United States was not founded as an experiment in cosmopolitan democracy but as a European, or more accurately an English, experiment in republicanism.

Men may have been created equal, but this equality said nothing of their abilities. Men were equal in the eyes of God and equal in their dignity; no man had the right to enslave another as a permanent political subject. This was the founders' understanding of men being "created equal." In all other respects, such as physical attributes, natural talents, inclinations, dispositions, abilities, and opportunities, men are unequal.

Proponents of the "propositional nation" would have you believe that America is an abstraction—a set of principles that anyone can adopt if they so choose, and in doing so, become as American as anyone else. They point to America's long history of immigration as evidence of this belief.

To be fair, there is some truth to this. America has a long history of successfully welcoming waves of immigrants into her arms. However, what they fail to mention is that the immigrants of the past often shared a common culture. They were Europeans, with whom we shared similar customs and beliefs, and whose histories were tied to ours through a common origin. In short, they were family.

And that is what a nation is, a family. The word "nation" comes from the Old French "nacion," meaning birth, rank, descendants, relatives, and homeland. Nacion comes from the Latin word "nationem," which means "birth, origin; breed, stock, tribe or race." Nationem translates directly to "that which has been born," or in Old Latin "gnasci." And "gnasci" traces its origin to the Proto-Indo-European root gene- meaning "give birth, or beget."

A nation is a family, and any addition to a family from the outside, regardless of relation, can be challenging. Anyone who is married knows that each family possesses its own idiosyncrasies—unspoken customs and ways of doing things that remain unseen until someone from outside the family points them out. These peculiarities are easily overcome when husband and wife share the same culture, but they become more challenging as the cultures become more alien.

America was able to thrive with the illusion of the propositional nation because she was adopting her cousins. She was welcoming her extended family, and although the particulars of their cultures caused tensions, they shared the same origin, and the same spirit, and this made integration possible. Catholic immigration from Italy, Ireland, and Germany presented challenges, but they were challenges that could be overcome. Protestants and Catholics might argue about how to celebrate Christmas, but at the end of the day, they both celebrate Christmas.

In addition to a shared cultural origin, the influx of immigrants was often slow and diffused over a wide area. German, Jewish, and Catholic immigrants to the South arrived slowly and in small numbers and as a result, were absorbed into the culture. They became Southerners, distinguished only by where they went to church on Sunday. This assimilation stands in stark contrast to large cities like New York where ethnic enclaves became the norm, allowing immigrants, despite a shared root culture, to wall themselves off and avoid integration.

Despite a shared cultural origin, the adoption of Western European immigrants still altered the nation. Change is an inevitable result of immigration and America understood the danger this posed to the soul of the nation, especially the danger posed by large numbers of unassimilated immigrants. The Immigration Act of 1924 placed a permanent numerical limit on immigration, added a national-origin quota system, and limited annual immigration to 150,000 persons. According to the Department of State, the purpose of the act was “to preserve the ideal of U.S. homogeneity.

There were numerous changes to U.S. immigration policy in the following years, but it was the Immigration and Nationality Act of 1965 (Hart-Celler Act) that would dramatically alter the face of America.

The Hart-Celler Act removed the National Origins Formula that was established in 1924 to preserve American homogeneity. Before Hart-Celler, the U.S. was 85% White, with Blacks making up 11%, and Latinos less than 4%. If the bill and its subsequent immigration waves had not been passed, it is estimated that the U.S. would have been in 2015: 75% Non-Hispanic White, 14% Black, 8% Hispanic, and less than 1% Asian American.

In America today, Whites make up 58% of the population, Blacks 12.4%, and Hispanics 19%. This massive demographic change represents a shift in the soul of the nation. America was born out of the English tradition, with values of private property, freedom of speech, and religious liberty tracing their origins to English Common Law. English Common Law itself was born of the Magna Carta and Roman Law. America is a nation deeply rooted in these historical and cultural foundations, and this foundation is a result of the people from which it was built.

As Hamilton wrote,

> *The safety of a republic depends essentially on the energy of a common National sentiment; on a uniformity of principles and habits; on the exemption of the citizens from foreign bias and prejudice; and on that love of country which will almost invariably be found to be closely connected with birth, education and family.*[56]

The founders understood that America was what she was because of who she was. People are not interchangeable; they are not isolated beings that can be molded to fit any system. A culture presupposes a people because the culture is the expression of the soul of a people. Just as each individual's soul differs, so too does the soul of each people. This is not a value judgment but a statement of fact. Does anyone truly believe that if you replaced the Chinese with Englishmen, they could have built the Han Dynasty? Or that if the Founding Fathers were Peruvian, America would look anything like it does today?

Changing a people fundamentally changes a nation because the collective identity, values, and traditions of a society are deeply rooted in its populace. The unique experiences, historical contexts, and intrinsic characteristics of a people shape their social structures, governance, and cultural expressions. When a different group with its own distinct heritage and worldview takes the place of the original inhabitants, the nation inevitably transforms to reflect the new group's identity. This shift alters everything from laws and institutions to art and customs, because the essence of a nation is inseparably linked to the people who reside within it.

America is not the same because the people are not the same. In the past, we adopted members of our extended family and while we differed in expression we shared the same cultural soul.

Today we invite the world into our home and act shocked when they turn it into a hotel. They do not care about our monuments or our heroes, they do not understand our traditions, or respect our laws. You will not find their names among the dead at Gettysburg or Belleau Wood, and when the barbarians descend upon this once great nation you will not find them standing by your side, because they will not fight what they let in.

> *...foreigners will generally be apt to bring with them attachments to the persons they have left behind; to the country of their nativity, and to its particular customs and*

manners. It is unlikely that they will bring with them that temperate love of liberty, so essential to real republicanism.
-Alexander Hamilton

[32]

A Different Shade of Blue: The Enduring Legacy of the Old South

There is no doubt about the atomizing and deracinating nature of modernity. Whether intentional or not, the spirit of the age is one that reduces man to interchangeable cogs in an industrial machine, separated by superficial prepackaged distinctions that can be purchased at the local big box retailer. The core characteristics of what separates us are fading, regional accents have been relegated to isolated rural communities and replaced by a generalized American accent, transmitted through smartphones to every corner of the country. Unique culinary dishes formed from local ingredients and customs have given way to the one size fits universal fast food. Even the stories we tell about ourselves have been altered to fit a homogenizing educational curriculum hand down from on high, straight from the halls of Washington.

Henry Ford once said, " You can get it (Model – T) in any color you want as long as it's black", and in America, you can have any regional distinction you want as long as it can be bought and sold at Walmart. It's a depressing realization, the loss of culture and identity. As Christ said, " For what does it profit a man to gain the world and lose his soul"; however, staring up at my grandparent's porch its ceiling paint colored in haint blue I realized that all was not lost.

For those that don't know "Haint blue", is a distinct shade of blue unique to the South, a color that predates the founding of America. The specific hue was originally made from crushed indigo and used by the Gullah, African slaves living in Georgia and South Carolina to paint the ceiling of their slave quarters, which they believed would ward off evil spirits or "haints". Over time the cultural cross-pollination facilitated by the close proximity of whites and blacks resulted in the adoption of haint blue as a Southern tradition. Porches decorated in blue became customary across the South.

It is in that color that I find hope. My Grandparent's house is new, built within the last two years. It is a product of modernity, its trimmings and appliances, mass-produced goods found in stores across the country, and its layout and architecture are contemporary and en vogue. There is nothing that sets their dwelling apart from a home in New York or Colorado, nothing except haint blue, that Southern color bleeding over from the past and staining the new.

Despite the attempts to uproot and erase our heritage as Southerners there lies a shade of blue that speaks to the enduring legacy of our culture. In time the American Empire will fade and with it the homogenizing power it wields. Southern culture will rise as the tide of Americanization recedes. So dye your ceilings blue and tell your boys about Bobby Lee, cause one day the carpetbaggers will have to leave, and though our accents may sound a little different, you will still find porches where men drink sweet tea under the protection of haint blue.

The past is never dead. It's not even past. -William Faulkner

[33]

Robert E Lee, MLK and Metagame Stagnation

My mind rebels at stagnation. Give me problems, give me work, give me the most abstruse cryptogram, or the most intricate analysis, and I am in my own proper atmosphere. But I abhor the dull routine of existence. I crave for mental exaltation.

-Arthur Conan Doyle

When I entered grade school in the early 90's, I unknowingly stepped onto an ideological battlefield that neither my parents nor I were aware of. Two god-like figures represented this conflict: Robert E. Lee on one side and Martin Luther King Jr. on the other. Surprisingly, until the late 2010s, most rural schools in Alabama celebrated Robert E. Lee Day each year on the third Monday in January, coinciding with MLK Day. Despite appearing to be a recipe for disaster, black and white students celebrated their respective holidays with little friction, thanks to an unspoken agreement that transpired with few incidents.

However, as I grew older, Robert E. Lee's legacy began fading. The public school system discreetly pushed him into the background while simultaneously elevating MLK to the status of a demigod. It was an ideological war that only one side was fighting, and by the time supporters of Robert E. Lee realized what was happening, it was too late. When I entered high school, the cult of MLK had reached its zenith. He had been elevated as the ideal American, the fulfillment of the American dream. Each year, we were subjected to an onslaught of MLK propaganda that portrayed him as the embodiment of the American ethos, representing everything the founders meant when they said, "All men are created equal," with all his virtues exalted and his vices forgotten.

Nevertheless, the deification of MLK was short-lived, and by the time I entered college, he had outlived his usefulness for the left. As the left became more radical, they began replacing MLK with figures who espoused more extreme views, such as Malcolm X and Angela Davis. These new icons better aligned with the left's evolving agenda, which prioritized identity politics and critical race theory over an astroturfed version of MLK's message of equality and unity. Consequently, MLK's legacy was left vulnerable, creating an opportunity for conservatives to claim the perceived moral high ground.

With MLK's legacy in the gutter, conservatives seized the opportunity to claim him as their own. The following decade saw a barrage of conservative talking heads lamenting the fact that MLK would have voted Republican if he were still alive. Conservatives' adoption of MLK was done without the slightest consideration for his many flaws, which, in all fairness, were heavily downplayed or outright hidden. With the victory of MLK's legacy over Robert E. Lee, MLK became the darling of mainstream conservatives par excellence. Predictably this proved to be a losing strategy, one conservatives would cling to despite its complete lack of effectiveness.

The game of, "we are the true fulfillment of MLK's legacy" seemed inescapable until a younger generation of the American Right rose to prominence. In game theory, when a game or sport has been completely figured out and no further strategic or technical advancements are possible within its rule set, the game is considered solved. For generations, the left had solved the game of equality propaganda. They would elevate a radical left icon until they reached a point of cultural normalcy, conservatives would attempt to repurpose them, and the left would discard them in favor of a new and more radical icon. This cycle would repeat time and again, shifting the discourse to the left each time.

This was a pattern the right seemed doomed to repeat in some Trotsky-esque perpetual revolution.

American conservatives had fallen into meta-game stagnation, adopting a single strategy with no room for strategic advancement or improvement. That was until a younger generation of right-wing thinkers emerged. This younger generation, "the new right," was freed from the monopolistic propaganda that once dominated the American psyche. The internet had provided access to a wealth of lost and forgotten information, leaving the new right free to explore and engage with ideas both old and new. For the first time in nearly a century, the right was able to break free from their ideological dead spin.

The response to MLK Day 2025 is a prime example of this. In the past, one would expect to see a tidal wave of pro-MLK sentiment, with the right trying to prove their ownership and the left passively paying their respects. While the left continued with its usual tactics, the dominant voice on the new right was a twofold response of apathy and counter-signaling.

The new right's apathy and counter-signaling toward MLK Day 2025 can be attributed to their access to alternative sources of information and their disillusionment with the establishment's narrative. Through the Internet, they discovered the complexities of MLK's character and how his legacy had been manipulated by both the left and the right. This newfound knowledge, coupled with a growing dissatisfaction with the status quo, emboldened the new right to challenge the established discourse and propose alternative philosophies.

Some on the new right chose to ignore MLK altogether, while others offered counter-icons, most notably Robert E. Lee and Stonewall Jackson. This wasn't merely an internet phenomenon; it was a tangible attack, culminating with the announcement that Mississippi and Alabama would reinstate Robert E. Lee Day. The left's response was toothless and quiet, passing with little to no effect outside their increasingly small sphere of influence.

This signals a shift in the game, leaving the left in a state of meta-game stagnation. The challenge for the right is to continue pushing forward without falling into the delusion that the game has been solved. This can only be achieved by a willingness to remain open to and adopt new strategies while avoiding the meta-game stagnation that plagues those who find themselves on the winning side.

[34]

The Leash and the Dollar

All we ask is to be left alone – Jefferson Davis

This past weekend, I had the luxury of attending the Old Glory Club conference in Memphis. The event was highlighted by a series of fantastic speakers, including Steven Carson, Jeff Deist, the Prudentialist, and many others. Among them was Auron Macintyre, whose recent book, "The Total State," is more than worth your time. On Saturday night, I had the pleasure of having dinner with Auron. We had a productive conversation about the state of modern education and Florida's school choice legislation. During our conversation, Auron made a profound statement: "The future is going to belong to the states that decouple themselves from federal funding."

Auron's statement was in response to my question about whether schools that accept money from the state of Florida would retain control over their curriculum. Fortunately for Floridians, their legislation specifically prohibits the state from dictating the curriculum for schools that receive state funds.

The question of state funding and school autonomy is a major concern of mine because Alabama has recently passed a very similar education program. This program would allow students who are withdrawn from public schools and placed in private schools to receive up to $7,000 in tuition paid by the state. After reviewing the Alabama School Choice Act (also known as the CHOOSE Act), it turns out that the Alabama Accountability Act is specifically designed to keep the state out of the business of telling schools what to teach. This setup mirrors the Florida model, aiming to provide educational choice while preserving curriculum independence.

Coercion via federal funding, as many of you may know, is one of the major tools of the federal government. There's no better example than the raising of the drinking age from 18 to 21. The federal government could not force states to change the drinking age directly; however, they leveraged federal highway funds to compel states to accept the new drinking age. Regardless of one's opinion on the appropriate legal drinking age, you can see the problem inherent in reliance on federal money. It's essentially a leash, and if you stray too far, Uncle Sam can yank it.

Another example is the federal No Child Left Behind Act, which tied federal education funds to specific performance metrics. Schools and states that did not comply with these metrics risked losing crucial funding, forcing many to align with federal standards even if they disagreed with them. Similarly, the Affordable Care Act used federal Medicaid funds to push states toward expanding Medicaid coverage, illustrating yet again how federal dollars come with strings attached.

In my last article, I discussed the process of catabolic collapse that the American Empire is experiencing. The main point was that as the federal government's grip begins to slip, states will be able to reassert their autonomy. This newfound independence will be much easier to achieve without the leash of federal funds tying them down. The states that stand to benefit the most from this reduction in federal power are the ones that are able to begin the process of decoupling themselves now. The fact is that the biggest tool the federal government has is not the military but the purse.

The path forward clearly lies in independence, with states becoming as self-reliant as possible. This is easier said than done, as breaking away from something one is addicted to is never easy. The question then becomes: how do we encourage states to divorce themselves from their addiction to federal dollars? One approach could be to gradually reduce dependence on federal funds by diversifying state revenue sources and encouraging local solutions to local problems. Additionally, states could form regional coalitions to share resources and best practices, lessening the need for federal intervention.

Ultimately, the move towards state self-reliance is a challenging but necessary journey. It requires strong leadership, committed citizens, and a willingness to innovate and collaborate. By fostering a culture of independence and resilience, states can reclaim their autonomy and better serve their populations.

[35]

Catabolic Opportunity

Dear reader, I am just as tired of the endless stream of theories as I'm sure you are. I have done my best over the last year to turn my focus on pragmatic real-world solutions. Yet, I ask that you bear with me as I add yet another theory to your plate. But trust me in the wake of this theory opportunity lies.

A few years back, the theory of Catabolic Collapse was garnering attention as a lens through which to understand the dynamics of societal decline. The theory originated from John Michael Greer's essay *How Civilizations Fall: A Theory of Catabolic Collapse.*[57] Greer's theory posits that civilizations face the risk of gradual disintegration due to the compounding effects of resource depletion, diminishing returns on investments, and societal complexities. In essence it is the gradual degradation of a civilization due to rising maintenance cost.

It's like when a company keeps investing in new projects, but they don't bring in as much profit as before. Over time, the company starts using up its resources faster than it can replenish them. To cope, it has to cut costs by reducing services or laying off employees. This downward spiral weakens the company's ability to function, leading to further declines until it can't sustain itself anymore. Similarly, catabolic collapse suggests that civilizations face a similar fate when they can't maintain their complex systems and infrastructure due to resource scarcity and diminishing returns on their efforts. This can lead to societal breakdowns and eventual collapse if the challenges aren't addressed effectively.

These "catabolic processes," wherein societies cannibalize their existing infrastructure and institutions to sustain themselves in the face of declining resources, can be seen in America today. The aging infrastructure, economic inequality, environmental degradation, inefficient healthcare system, and political polarization collectively reflect the strains of sustaining complex systems with limited resources.

Greer's collapse is a bit hyperbolic and is best described as an explanation of social decline. Catabolic Collapse is a stair-step model wherein catastrophic events are followed by periods of stabilization. These stable periods last until the resources acquired from catabolizing run out and the process repeats. As overplayed as the example of the collapse of the Roman Empire is, it is especially prescient here. Rome did not collapse into a Mad Max-style free-for-all; rather, its sphere of influence slowly waned as those on the fringes realized the Empire's reach no longer extended to them.

It's this receding tide of influence that is most interesting to us. If Greer's theory holds true, then we can expect to see the American Empire step back as it can no longer afford to maintain control of its vassals. Texas Governor Greg Abbott's (la'anatu 'llahi 'alay-hi) recent challenge of federal immigration policy seems to be a sign of just this. Although nothing substantial materialized out of Abbott's challenge, the fact that the federal government did nothing speaks volumes. Thirty years ago, they burned Waco to the ground; today, they allowed a challenge to their authority to go nearly unopposed.

For us, this presents a powerful opportunity. Much has been said about the merits of local political action, and that option has never looked better than it does now. Local political victories today have the potential to become exponentially powerful. As the federal government continues to cede power to the states, local municipalities will become increasingly influential. As the finance bros say, "buy low, sell high."

I expect we will see the federal government relinquishing control and states asserting greater autonomy with ever-increasing frequency. This certainly guarantees that local political action will become increasingly influential. With this shift in power dynamics, opportunities for impactful change burgeon at the grassroots level. Now is the time to recognize the potential of local victories, as municipalities rise in prominence and wield greater authority. As catabolic collapse continues to chip away at federal power, positions of authority will be ours for the taking—you just have to get off the couch and do something.

[36]

Friends and Enemies:The Symbology of Trump

When the oak is felled the whole forest echoes with its fall, but a hundred acorns are sown in silence by an unnoticed breeze.
-Thomas Carlyle

Saturday night I was at dinner with my wife and some friends when the news about Trump's attempted assassination broke. Seeing the reaction of those around me reminded me that Trump was more than just a presidential candidate. He is a symbol, and the people love him. They love Trump because for the first time in their lives someone is speaking for them, he represents Americans from deindustrialized towns, farming communities and flyover states. And it is for this very reason that those in power, hate him, they hate him because they despise everyday average Americans, they hate him because they hate us.

The elites do not care about us. They have no problem gutting the manufacturing base and sending our jobs overseas, flooding our towns with fentanyl, and replacing us with Third World immigrants. They see us as a problem, a thorn in their side, a nuisance that needs to be dealt with.

Subscribed

For all his faults Trump had the audacity to stand up for us. It's ironic because Trump is not one of us, he's the last person one might expect to stand for the American heart land. He is a real estate mogul, a billionaire, and he's from New York City, he's about as far from everyday America as one can get. But this only makes the powers that be hate him more—because he's one of them. He always has been. He went to the same parties, funded their campaigns, and at the end of the day, he dared to turn against them. Trump is more than just a political nuisance for the establishment. He's far worse than that. He is a heretic. He is a traitor.

He dared to stand up to them and stand up for us. We can argue till we're blue in the face about Trump's politics. I will be the first to admit he is not someone with whom I share many political beliefs. But he is a friend, and if there's one thing, we have learned since 2016 it's that Carl Schmitt was absolutely right. Politics is about friends and enemies.

The line between friend-enemy was made clear on

July 13. There is no longer any ambiguity to be found. Conspiracies aside, there is one fact that remains: the rooftop from which the shooter fired on Trump was left unsecured, and there is zero reason that should've happened. The only logical explanation is that it was done intentionally because they wanted everyone to see his brain turned to pink mist on live television.

They wanted us to see that because they wanted us to understand our place. They wanted us to realize that this is not our country anymore. They're in charge, and we need to sit down, shut up, and go back to politics as it once existed—to continue to choose between a false binary, a ruling party and a controlled opposition.

They wanted him dead, and they wanted it televised because they wanted to send a message. That message is clear: they hate us. They hate us for not sitting by and watching as they raid the treasury, as they demographically replace us, as they send our sons to die in far-off lands.

We were supposed to sit down and shut up, and if we're being honest, that is what most of us were doing until Trump. Trump had the audacity to expose them for who they are, to turn against them, and to rally those states they deemed flyover country and offer them hope.

Regardless of his policies, or whether you agree with him, it is undeniable that he has rejuvenated the average American's believe that they might control their own destiny. He has given us a vitality that had long been dormant. We watched over the last couple of years as Republicans and right-leaning people won victories at the state level, became active in school boards, county commissions, and mayor's offices. These political victories were largely because Trump exposed them for who they are, and by shedding light their intentions and exposing the cancer that is Washington he reinvigorated a people who had previously resigned their country to vultures.

The establishment hates Trump because he represents the average American, he represents you and me, he represents our families and our communities. They want him out of the way because they want us out of the way. He was supposed to lay down and step aside because we were supposed to lay down and step aside. They wanted him dead because they want us dead.

Regardless of my political disagreements with President Trump, he now has my full support. When those coastal elites look at him, they don't just see a brash, loud New York real estate executive with eccentric hair. They see factory workers from Ohio, they see fishermen from the coast of North Carolina, they see farm boys from Iowa. They see Americans, and they hate us.

[37]

Take What the Defense Gives You

If you've ever stepped onto a football field, chances are you've heard your coach hammering one phrase into your skull: "take what the defense gives you." It's like a mantra, a guiding principle that's supposed to navigate you through the chaos of the game. And it's pretty self-explanatory, really. But just for the sake of clarity, let's break it down: when your opponent slips up, makes a mistake, or unwittingly cedes territory, you pounce. You seize the opportunity laid out before you with both hands and make the most of it.

During the recent chaos unfurling across college campuses, surrounding subject of Israel and Palestine, a single photograph emerged, capturing a group of white fraternity brothers standing guard around the American flag. This image spread, like wildfire, engulfing the attention everyone on the political right, from the standard-issue Fox News conservatives to seasoned veterans of the Dissident Right.

To many, it wasn't just a picture; it was a beacon of hope, a small white pill, a drop of water in the desert of ideological warfare.

Like clockwork, the counter-signaling commenced. Accounts across Twitter (X) began their usual routine of "Actually," followed by attempts to educate their followers on why this was a misguided gesture. They aimed to redirect the narrative towards the "real" story. But you and I both know that in the grand scheme of things, the truth of a matter often takes a backseat to its spirit.

Now, I can empathize with the inclination to highlight the inconvenient truth that the flag these young men are staunchly defending represents, in large part, a government that hates them. It symbolizes a regime that actively undermines their ability to become the men God indented them to be. A regime that is intent on snipping their threads in the fabric of society by squeezing them out of the job market, precipitating economic downturns, and auctioning off their birthright piece by piece.

All of that holds true, but it's crucial to bear in mind that the flag isn't synonymous with the government it represents. For many on the right, particularly those entrenched in mainstream conservative circles, the flag holds profound significance. It's not merely a symbol of governance but rather intertwined with notions of heritage, home, and personal identity. It embodies their sense of belonging and self.

With that in mind, our focus shouldn't solely dwell on the government's actions but also on the instincts driving these young men to safeguard the flag. They're acting in accordance with a primal urge, defending what they perceive as theirs, and that impulse is something we should endorse. Granted, these instincts might be misdirected, but at their core, they represent a sense of loyalty and honor.

Every individual, within the Dissident Right, started somewhere. If we're honest with ourselves, many of us can trace our paths back to where these young men currently stand. That instinct to shield one's flag and people resonates deeply—it's a sentiment that in part drove me to enlist in the Marine Corps. Evolving from the position these young men occupy now to where the DR is today, is a journey that takes time and reflection.

There's little merit in hastily rushing to countersignal these young men. At their core, their intentions are noble—they embody the type of individuals we want standing alongside us. Instead of immediately pushing back against their actions, we should seize this opportunity to engage with them, to introduce them to our ideas. After all, you catch more flies with honey.

Ultimately, if we aim to enact meaningful change, we must prioritize building relationships and forging alliances. Just as in football where you're taught to take what the defense gives you, in our interactions with these young men, we should see their willingness to defend the flag as an opportunity. We need to make ourselves approachable to those who may not yet align entirely with our beliefs. These young men are already on the right path; they just might need a gentle push in the right direction. Like leading a horse to water, we can't fault them for not immediately drinking.

[38]

Utopians All the Way Down

U.S. District Judge Sharon Johnson Coleman recently ruled that illegal immigrants can exercise their Second Amendment rights and legally own guns in the U.S. It doesn't take much to see the fault in the decision. There is no scenario where arming a flood of military-aged third-world males plays out well. Regardless, this has not stopped Libertarians from signaling their status as Second Amendment absolutists.

This absolutist dedication to rights is a prime example of the naiveté that plagues the Libertarian movement. They are functionally no different from Communists. That may seem absurd, but one must consider that both Communists and Libertarians are utopian idealists whose ideology cannot properly account for human nature.

Both see humans as rational beings who will act in

their own best interests given the proper incentive structure. The fundamental flaw in this is that there is no universal rational; in the abstract, perhaps, but for humans, it is subjective.

The vast majority of people do not make logical, objective decisions; rather, they post hoc rationalize their desires. The rational faculty is simply a tool of justification. You will find this on display with a trip to any Walmart: masses of morbidly obese individuals filling their carts with coke and Oreos, slowly killing themselves. They are surrounded by healthy options that any rational actor should prioritize. In theory, one should expect that health and nutrition would be primary, yet in reality, it takes a backseat to momentary mouth pleasure.

I have no doubt that many Libertarians mean well; they truly believe that their ideology will result in the best of all possible worlds. This naive utopianism leaves them open to exploitation by more nefarious actors, as Jonathan Bowden points out in his speech on *Marxism and the Frankfurt School*.

> *In all Marxist groups you get the rather weak, pacifistic, loving, humanistic people. The vicar's daughter who believes human nature isn't . . . right. If only we could be nicer to each other, if only we could spread more love. You get these people always in ultra-Left and Communist groups, and next to them on the podium, next to them in the auditorium, [are] your utterly nihilistic, ruthless, virtually criminal types who want to use the structure of power when they get it to crush those underneath them, don't give a damn about ideology, and are actually amongst the most misanthropic people you*

could ever meet. And you have these extremes of the innocent lovey and the sort of sadistic amoralist in the same group." – Johnathan Bowden

For every well-meaning Libertarian on stage next to them is a cartoonishly greedy mega- corporation waiting to exploit a lack of regulations and kneecap every mom-and-pop shop in the country.

Libertarianism is an ideology that deals with the world as it "ought" to be and not as it is. If there is one thing the right must learn, it is that we must deal with political reality. Power will be used by our enemies whether we like it or not. To throw our hands up in some moralistic plea for liberty is foolish.

I have a lot of love for Libertarians; they are mostly good people with good instincts, but it's time for them to grow up.

[39]

Youth and Young Manhood

[40]

Embrace the Suck

A few months ago, Cremieux shared a Twitter thread analyzing data related to the ongoing veteran suicide crisis (you can find the thread here). In his analysis, Cremieux emphasizes that there is no predisposition of suicidal individuals entering the military, nor is there a connection between combat experience, PTSD, and suicide. This information may come as a shock, as most Americans tend to assume that the epidemic of suicides in the military is a side effect of combat experience. However, this could not be further from the truth. The reality is that the suicide problem has less to do with the military and more to do with who's in the military because the suicide problem is a demographic issue. It just so happens that the demographic making up the bulk of suicides also makes up the bulk of the U.S. military. The hard truth is suicide is a male problem and more specifically a "White male problem."

As stated above, this is not an issue of trauma or PTSD; rather, it is an issue of purpose. Young men (and men in general) have watched their roles in society be replaced by the state and technology. They are no longer needed to perform the basic functions that men have provided since Adam was expelled from the garden. Everywhere they turn, they are told that they are dysfunctional, maladjusted, and the future is female.

This process of replacement has been occurring for the better part of a century. For years, male-only spaces provided a reprieve, but over time, those have been co-opted or outright destroyed; just look at the Boy Scouts or sports. The longest-standing and most prolific male space, the military, has finally been usurped as well.

Traditionally, the military has provided young men with a sense of purpose or the perception of one. For those who may have been eager to join, the military is no longer a viable option, evident in the Department of Defense's inability to meet recruiting numbers. For those already enlisted, many are simply waiting to retire. So, what are they left with? A dead-end desk job, massive college debt, fentanyl?

When young men look to their future, they are confronted with a desolate landscape. There is nothing above them or below, nothing to strive for – just an empty expanse filled with cheap material goods and fleeting hedonistic pleasures to ward off meaninglessness. This sense of purposelessness disproportionately affects white men, given their inclination towards prioritizing delayed gratification and planning for the future. However, when the future appears devoid of purpose, what course of action remains?

As these young men look ahead and realize they have no community, culture, or control over their families (as their wives always have the option to leave and take everything), the future appears bleak, and it seems like nobody cares. Eventually, they rationalize that death is a preferable alternative.

I am all too familiar with the feeling.

[41]

Normie Maxing: When people respect you, they trust you

Dear reader,

It's been a while since I last wrote, and there are two reasons for my silence. Firstly, I haven't had much to say, and I tend to reserve my verbosity for face-to-face interactions rather than here. Secondly, I've been preoccupied with real-life endeavors, and hopefully, in the upcoming weeks, I'll have plenty to share with you in that regard.

With summer fast approaching, so too comes the seasonal downturn in political discourse and the shift toward more social activities and less formal engagement.

Given this, I urge you all to be as normal as possible. Summer brings a plethora of social opportunities, and if there's one area where many on the Dissident Right could use some practice, it's social interaction. Some of us may have grown accustomed to being the outsider, to being persona non grata. While there's a certain allure to that, at the end of the day, it's a net negative. You need to be relationship-maxing. One thing my experience in business has taught me is that all business relationships are friendships.

Networking often boils down to whether people like you or not. It's as simple as that. Therefore, it's crucial that you use the summer months to hone your social skills. If you really want to make a difference, if you want to change things, you're going to need some level of popular support, and the easiest way to get popular support is to be cool.

For some of you, being popular just comes naturally. It's something you're born with, as Bowden once said, "You can do a bit, but you're born to be what you are."

For those less socially inclined, don't worry. Social charm is something that can be learned and refined. So, allow me to offer a few tips to help you maximize your personal magnetism.

Firstly, appearance matters. While it's not everything, first impressions count. This means grooming, dressing well, and taking care of your physical health. Go find a barber; a haircut goes a long way. Dress well; if you are like me and have no fashion sense, ask your wife or girlfriend. If you're romantically challenged, find the least gay men's fashion channel on YouTube and take notes. While you're at it, put down the chicken nuggets and pizza and hit the gym.

Secondly, conversation is key. Being able to engage in a variety of topics will serve you well in social settings. Being a conversational generalist can help you navigate diverse social circles more easily. A jack of all trades will have a lot easier time navigating social functions than somebody who spends all their time talking about the logistical challenges faced by the Wehrmacht in 1931. That's just the way it is. It's great to have specialized knowledge, but you need to learn to keep your spaghetti in your pocket. You don't need to word vomit about Franco when you're hanging out by the pool with friends. You can save that for later.

Lastly, patronage is crucial. Building relationships based on mutual trust and reciprocity is essential. There has been a lot of talk about patronage in our circles, but patronage is more than just buying things from our guys. Patronage also means doing things for other people. Get involved in your local community, lend a helping hand, and make yourself known for your contributions.

So, here's your summer mission: become more personable and socially adept. If you want your ideas to gain traction, being someone others admire or enjoy being around is paramount. When people respect and trust you, they're more likely to be receptive to your ideas and perspectives.

Think of it as nobles oblige for the average Joe. You

have a responsibility to share truths with people, but those truths are more palatable when delivered by someone they like or aspire to be like.

Remember, everything you dislike about yourself is changeable. Whether it's weight, style, or social skills, improvement is within reach. So, get out there, attend social events, and engage with others. I love elite theory as much as the next anon, but we can't ignore the power of likability. After all, it's much easier to build and maintain power when people genuinely like you.

[42]

Perception and the Art of Reality: A Woman Simply is, but a Man Must Become

"Perception is reality," is an adage that communicates a fundamental truth about the world in which we live, that is—that which we perceive to be true is true, because truths are those things that are not simply acknowledged, but must be discovered, or created. In this case it is creation that we are concerned with, more specifically the creation of a perception, the creation of truth.

I have seen over the years an ever-increasing number of young men who are disillusioned with the dating market. For many of these young men the lack of romantic success is less their fault and more of a byproduct of the Zeitgeist. However, more often than not the young men I see complaining about the fancifully high standards of women are to put it bluntly losers.

But one need not remain a loser, as Camille Paglia said, “A woman simply is, but a man must become.” This means that if you are a loser, you became a loser and if you can become one thing you can become another.

This act of metamorphosis is simple and surprisingly easy, it only requires commitment and patience. That being the case I have decided to provide a step-by-step guide on how to create the perception needed to redefine your reality.

Step I: Foundation.

Before you continue reading, take a moment, step in front of the mirror and ask yourself, “Do I like what I see?” If the answer is no, congratulations you’re normal. If the answer is yes and you are not golden era Arnold then you’re a liar. The point is there is room for improvement. Beginning a workout routine can be daunting there is a lot of information out there and most of it is useless. What you need to know is women don’t expect you to look like Mr. Olympia in fact most women when asked said they prefer a physique similar to that of Brad Pitt in *Fight Club*. I won’t get into the details because there are too many variables to consider with each individual, but the steps are really the same.

- Get a gym membership.
- Find a Hypertrophy program. I recommend checking out Axios.[58]
- Lift 3 to 4 times a week.
- Throw out all of the processed food, shop the perimeter of the store and up your protein intake.

Step II: Wardrobe.

Building your body is one aspect; the subsequent step involves dressing the physique you've cultivated. Begin by discarding all cargo shorts and graphic tees you own—it's time to be a man. If you aim to avoid the label of a loser, it's crucial to cease dressing like one. Your wardrobe should align with your lifestyle; there's no merit in stocking up on three-piece suits if your daily environment involves working on an oil rig. To err on the side of practicality, I've compiled a basic list of essential items for a business casual day-to-day wardrobe.

Items that should be in the Business Casual Wardrobe:

- 1 Suit & 2 Ties (Just in case!)
- 1 Pair Dress Shoes
- 2 Pair Casual Leather Shoes (Suede or Saddle Shoes)
- Belts that match (above) shoes

- 10+ Dress Shirts (tailored, contrast stitching, unique fabrics)
- 4 Pairs of well-fitting Jeans
- 2 Pair Slacks, Dark & Light
- 6+ Button-up collared sport shirts
- 2 Solid Polo Shirts
- 6 Sweaters
- 10+ Undershirts
- 1+ Sports Jacket – unique style or fabric
- 1 Simple Watch
- 5+ Pocket Squares
- 1 Overcoat (Aim for a Unique Fabric)

Items that would be helpful to have/ but are not necessary.

- 2 Vests — possibly wear in lieu of a jacket.
- 1 pair of Leather Gloves
- 1 Hat
- Collar Stays, Cuff Links

Keep in mind that fit is paramount; a budget-friendly, well-tailored suit will outshine an expensive, off-the-rack counterpart. If you are working on a budget find a Goodwill or consignment shop in a rich neighborhood and you will often find like new designer clothing and with the money you save you can take it to a tailor.

Also, checkout The Art of Manliness[59] they have a plethora of articles regarding men's fashion that will provide a deeper understanding of what is required to dress like a man.

Step III: Knowledge.

I am sure there is a woman somewhere who finds encyclopedic knowledge of Warhammer 40K factions fascinating, but for most women, it will get you about as far as being a eunuch. The key is to be able to converse about many different topics, when it comes to conversation it is best to be a "jack of all trades." There is no better way to expand your knowledge and attention span than by reading. Personally, I prefer a fiction-nonfiction rotation. Considering the state of modern literature, I have provided a list of titles below that will be of value to any young man.

- The Brothers Karamazov by Fyodor Dostoevsky
- The Sun Also Rises by Ernest Hemingway
- Nicomachean Ethics by Aristotle
- The Iliad & The Odyssey by Homer
- A River Runs Through It by Norman Maclean
- The Count of Monte Cristo by Alexander

Dumas

- All Quiet on the Western Front by Erich Maria Remarque
- Lives by Plutarch
- The Bible
- Lonesome Dove by Larry McMurtry
- All the Pretty Horse by Cormac Mcarthy
- The Maltese Falcon by Dashiell Hammett
- All the Kings Men by Robert Penn Warren
- Leviathan by Thomas Hobbes
- Slaughterhouse-Five by Kurt Vonnegut

Step IV: Skill.

To understand the final step, it is important to understand what women want. While that is a loaded question that no one, not even women can answer, subconsciously it's simple. Women want security. While physical strength is a factor in today's world security is primarily a financial venture. Less mature men will call this gold-digging but in reality, women risk a lot by getting pregnant and they need safety and security in order to birth and raise children. One way women evaluate a man is based on potential and your career is a measure of potential par excellence. So, I will give the same advice I give my sons; consider either college or trade school, and let your aptitude guide your choice.

If college is your thing than you have to consider the Return on Investment (ROI) and growth potential. This will limit your options and in my opinion that means your choices are medical doctor, lawyer, engineering, or STEM more broadly.

If it's trade school than find a trade and take business classes on the side because the real money is not in the trade itself but owning the business that provides the trade.

Either path will increase your potential and to any sensible young woman potential is gold.

Step V: Live it.

This brings us full circle. Perception is reality, you are the master of your image, what you create is what the world sees. The truth of who you are is subject to your will. If you want to increase your success in life or in the dating market, you must be the architect of truth. With a little bit of pain and patience you can master perception and reality. If you build it, they will come.

[43]

Rodeo and Racing: The Virtue of Risk

A few weekends ago, I was watching Professional Bull Riding (PBR) with my oldest son and I couldn't shake the feeling that something was missing. Sure, there were cowboys, bulls, and rodeo clowns. It had all the elements of rodeo and yet it lacked something. It had no soul. The raw and rugged nature of the sport had been replaced by safety gear and commercial brakes. The danger inherent in rodeo had been removed and stripped away in the process of commodification in order to make it more palatable for a general audience.

Racing has faced a similar fate. Gone are the days of fiery explosions at Le Mans. There is no more Group B in Rally Racing or true stock car racing. The sport was once the domain of men who pushed the limits of man and machine. The same spirit that crossed oceans and conquered continents is the same spirit that animated drivers to risk everything for glory on the track. That is all gone, replaced by safety regulations that homogenize sport to the point that competitive advantage no longer exists in any meaningful way.

The obsession with safety has poisoned everything. Sure, we may have reduced injuries and fatalities but at what cost? The coddling and overprotective nature of our society has created weak and effeminate men. Each subsequent generation following the Boomers has become increasingly obsessed with nerfing the world. You can blame women or commercialization it doesn't matter, It's sad and pathetic.

The sense of danger and risk taking is a necessary element of the masculine spirit. It needs outlets. It needs rodeo, racing, and boxing, it needs adventure. Those things will never be safe, but the world isn't safe, and what kind of men do you want to raise? Do you want soft, weak men who have never taken risks, or do you want men that are willing to take on the world?

This country wasn't built by men who were scared of a bloody lip, and it won't be saved by the either.

[44]

Football American

There's a spirit, there's an energy, there's a passion in college football that you can't replicate anywhere else. It's about pride, tradition, and a love for the game.
– Pat Dye

I spent the weekend visiting friends in western North Carolina, reminiscing and taking stock of the damage caused by Hurricane Helene. I had forgotten it was Super Bowl weekend and didn't know who was playing. This isn't new for me—I didn't reject the NFL because of BLM or COVID. I never liked the NFL, never cared about the Super Bowl, and never will.

My dislike of professional football is not a hot take. I have never understood the appeal of an obviously commercialized and inorganic product like the NFL. What does it really mean to be a Cowboys or Raiders fan? What truly ties a professional sports franchise to a community? What roots, what genuine connection, can be found in a league where teams relocate at the whim of an owner chasing a better financial deal? The NFL, at its core, is nothing more than a mass-produced, corporate imitation of the greatest sport in America: college football.

Before the corrosive influence of NIL deals, the playoffs, and the transfer portal, college football embodied everything that made sports great. Its play style was regional, its players were local, and its history was deeply rooted in, and inseparable from, the fan base that supported it. College football was not just a game—it was an identity, a way of life that reflected the character of the communities it represented.

If the NFL is the epitome of the inorganic commodification of sports, then college football was its antithesis. It was a purely organic sport, rich with the unique flavor of the college towns that each team called home. When I was growing up, we dreamed of bowl season where we could witness the clash of vastly different styles—pass-happy West Coast teams facing off against the bruising, power-I juggernauts of the Deep South, or the corn-fed, heavy offensive lines of Nebraska taking on the suffocating defenses of the SEC. College football was a battleground of cultures, a national spectacle where Alabama vs. Penn State felt like a rematch of the Civil War and Notre Dame vs. Miami was Catholics vs. Convicts. These rivalries were not manufactured drama for TV ratings; they were built on decades—sometimes over a century—of real history and real stakes.

These regional differences weren't just arbitrary. They were the product of more than a hundred years of tradition. The oldest rivalry in college football, Yale vs. Princeton, has been played since 1873. Auburn and Georgia have clashed nearly every year since 1892. Minnesota and Wisconsin have played 134 times since 1890. Army and Navy have battled 125 times since 1890, and their rivalry remains one of the most meaningful spectacles in American sports.

It wasn't just the longevity of these rivalries that made them special, but their infrequency. Other sports boast heated rivalries with long and storied histories, but the nature of those competitions dilutes their significance. The Red Sox may lose to the Yankees, but they have another chance just a few weeks later. In college football, you get one game. One shot. One opportunity to claim bragging rights for an entire year. When Auburn plays Alabama or Ohio State plays Michigan, everything is on the line. A 5-6 season could be redeemed by winning the big one because that one game meant everything. And in an era before players were merely auditioning for the NFL, these teams—composed of local and regional players, many of whom were playing their last game—left everything on the field. This made college football rivalries some of the most electrifying games ever played.

The fan base was as organic as the rivalries

themselves. They were made up of alumni, the relatives of alumni, and those with a direct connection to the university. From these roots sprang traditions passed down for generations. Rolling Toomer's Corner at Auburn, Ralphie's run at Colorado, dotting the "i" at Ohio State, and touching Howard's Rock at Clemson—each school took pride in ceremonies so deeply embedded in tradition that their origins are sometimes lost to history. The connection between fans and their teams was not based on arbitrary loyalty to a brand or a logo; it was a birthright, a sacred bond between university, team, and town.

College football was everything that made sports great. It was organic. It was traditional. It was deeply rooted in the community. It was about pride—not in some corporate entity, but in something real, something personal.

Unfortunately, the ever-greedy eye of Sauron couldn't let college football's monetary potential remain untapped. In the last couple of years, everything that made college football special has been systematically dismantled. Coaches no longer stay for decades to build programs and legacies—now, they hop from school to school every few years in pursuit of a national championship and a fatter contract. Gone are the days of Bobby Bowden and Bear Bryant, icons who spent their entire careers (or close to it) shaping a single program.

The bowl system, ubiquitous with college football,

that unique post-season tradition that celebrated regional champions, has been replaced by a playoff system designed to squeeze more money out of the sport. More games mean more TV revenue. The NIL deals have turned players into mercenaries, less concerned with school pride and more focused on preserving their bodies for the NFL Draft. And the transfer portal ensures that rosters are in constant flux, as players jump from school to school in search of the most lucrative opportunity or easiest path to playing time.

The loss of the historical bowl system in favor of the playoffs has stripped college football of one of its most cherished traditions. The bowl games were once the crown jewel of the season, honoring conference champions and offering unique, tradition-laden matchups that were often the only time certain programs would ever meet. Each bowl had its own identity, from the Rose Bowl's historic Big Ten vs. Pac-12 clash to the Sugar Bowl's deep Southern roots.

These games were not just postseason exhibitions; they were milestones, marking yearly endpoints in the sport's history. Now, the focus has shifted entirely to the playoff, which prioritizes television ratings and corporate sponsorships over the pageantry and tradition that made college football special. The once-glorious bowl season has been relegated to a series of meaningless games, serving merely as consolation prizes for teams that failed to make it to the next round.

The old college football is dead. The regional identities that once defined the sport are disappearing. The rivalries are becoming less meaningful as conferences realign with no regard for tradition. Players no longer spend their careers at one school, making it harder for fans to form lasting connections with the athletes who wear their colors and coaches no longer define programs. The game has lost its soul, its heart, its very essence.

College football was once the last great bastion of pure, unfiltered sports passion. But as it succumbs to the forces of global commodification it becomes yet another corporate product, another soulless imitation of what was, it will be NFL lite, a safe corporatized surrogate activity and I won't be there to watch.

College football isn't just a game; it's a part of the fabric of American culture, and the passion that surrounds it is what makes it special.

-Nick Saban

[45]

Technology and Technique

[46]

John Henry vs AI: Or How I learned to Embrace Technology

John Henry was an American Folk hero, a man who spent his days working on the railroad as a steel driver. His legend was born around the end of the 19th century, during the heart of the Second Industrial Revolution. New technology was being created at an unprecedented pace, and steam and electric power were allowing industrialization to change every facet of society. John Henry would come face to face with these new machines and the changes they brought. John Henry responded to those changes; according to legend to prove his might John Henry challenged a steam-powered rock-drilling machine to a race... and won. For his victory, he was immortalized, his story recorded in ballads so old the songwriter's identity has been lost to time.

When they invented that old steam drill
They thought that they had 'em somethin' fine
John Henry sank her fourteen feet
Steam drill only made her nine, Lord
Steam drill only made her nine

On the surface, the Legend of John Henry seems nothing more than a fun tale about a man so strong he could best a steam-powered engine, but it's not that simple. At its core, John Henry's story is a 19th-century formulation of the archetypal theme of man vs machine. It's the story of resistance to technological change and the fear of being replaced. John Henry lived during a time when technology was reshaping every aspect of life in America; so opposition to these changes naturally sprang up not only in America but across the Atlantic as well.

In England, new technology was met with violence. The Luddites are famous for destroying textile machines in the early part of the 19th century. The group was made up of individuals that felt displaced by this new technology, many of whom were factory owners who could not compete with the low prices produced by the new machine mills. They were the casualties of new tech, men, and women displaced and lashing out. The Luddites eventually engaged in a full-fledged revolt that required military intervention. and in the end, their violent opposition to technological change was crushed and did little to slow industrialization.

John Henry's story ends in a similar fashion. His triumph against the steam engine is a pyrrhic victory. After besting the machine Henry collapses from exhaustion and dies. Neither his victory nor his death matter, the machine marches on.

Both John Henry and the Luddites are reactions to a rapidly changing world. They display a fear of new technology. It is a fear particularly prevalent to those on the right; it's only natural for individuals who fancy themselves paleo-conservative, monarchist, traditionalist, or reactionaries to be skeptical or even outright hostile to technological change. After all, it threatens to uproot and change everything we love. It may be tempting to make reference to the Butlerian Jihad or the armies of Mordor or to refer back to *Industrial Society and its Future*, but what benefit is there in rejecting technology?

If you choose violent opposition you end up like the Samurai. The Meiji Restoration threatened their way of life and in the face of this threat, they chose war. Five hundred Samurai stood against thirty thousand Imperial troops at Shimoyama; they fought with honor yet in the end they were crushed by the industrial might of the Imperial Japanese Army. No amount of tradition or adherence to the Bushido code would see the sword triumph over the rifle. They simply gave their enemies a monopoly on new technology and for that, they paid with their lives.

If you choose to stand and prove your might as John Henry did you will share his fate. You may not die but you won't win in the long run; just ask Garry Kasparov how one victory over Deep Blue turned out. A temporary victory over the machine matters not. Technology will step over you and you will be washed away by the tide of "progress".

This is not to say that we should embrace technology blindly, rather we should understand technology as a tool, and like any tool, its potential for abuse should be recognized. Transhumanism, AI, digital currency, etc. there are plenty of reasons to be wary of new technology, but we should be mindful of these threats and not turn away from tech wholeheartedly. It is not acceptance or rejection but discernment that will win the future.

In the end, John Henry's story is a lesson in futility... the futility of rejecting new technology. It may be that an exercise in dialects is necessary to understand the proper synthesis between our natural world and the ever-advancing wave of technology. How we will integrate something like AI into our lives without losing our humanity is a challenge that is rapidly approaching.

What is certain is the time is coming when technology will render it so we will not be able to believe anything we see or hear. I for one do not look forward to that but I know that if we choose to reject that technology it will be turned against us and we will be left defenseless.

[47]

The Technological Tide Instinct: Intellect, and Dasein

Growing up in a rural community, nature was an ever-present companion. Regular encounters with the ebb and flow of life, from its wondrous genesis to its inevitable culmination, provided a profound backdrop for understanding life's essence in its most unfiltered form. The agony and glory of birth were witnessed, while the inevitability of death was reluctantly acknowledged. Yet, the relentless tide of urbanization has confined the vast majority of people to an endless sprawl of concrete and asphalt. Midst this artificial milieu, humanity finds itself severed from its roots, and life transforms into a mere semblance of its former self, a distant echo of what once was.

Without the frequent interaction with nature provided by rural and agricultural life, man relinquishes his understanding of the natural world. He becomes coddled and sheltered by an artificial urban existence that systematizes life and reduces the world to abstract concepts; birth becomes choice, a secondary function of the sexual faculty, relationships become transactional, and food is divorced from its source until meat stands entirely free from its true cost. In this urban domain, the instinct atrophies, and man, being of two natures—rational and instinctual—forsakes one at the cost of the other.

In *The Decline and Fall of the West* Oswald Spengler contrasted two fundamental aspects of human behavior: the instinctual and the intellectual[60]. For Spengler Instinct represents the more primal, intuitive, and deeply ingrained aspects of human nature, while intellect refers to the rational, analytical, and conscious thinking capacities. According to Spengler, during the early stages of a culture's development, instincts play a dominant role in shaping its values, beliefs, and actions. However, as a culture reaches its peak and transitions into its decline, intellect gains prominence. This shift from an instinctual to an intellectual focus is seen as a characteristic of the later stages of civilization, as rationality and analytical thinking become more emphasized.

We can best understand the relationship between instinct and intellect as analogous to space and time. Consider the earth at the dawn of a new year when the planet begins its orbit around the sun, the year counts down (time) while the distance the earth travels (space) increases. In this sense, we can say that time gives birth to space and space gives death to time. When a civilization is born, instinct (time) is its driving force, but as it grows, its intellect (space) increases and gradually surpasses, and in the end, completely overshadows the instinct.

It is in the later phase of this cycle that man becomes hyper-rational. To paraphrase Nietzsche, "The Greeks had two choices: become absurdly rational or die." This is because, in the late stages of civilization, people can no longer call back to their instinct, in the same way, a naval captain of today could not cross the Atlantic with a ship from the 18th century. The old ways are lost, and to return to them would be death.

It is when instinct and intellect are at equilibrium that man is at his best, open to his intuition and guided by the rational mind. Without this balance, man loses sight of reality, nature is a force to be tamed and exploited and life becomes a problem that requires a solution, Man commences to destroying himself and his world. He builds great machines that shelter him from nature eventually cutting himself off from God and meaning, he becomes the architect of his own demise.

This self-destructive drive is couched in the language of progress, and this "progress" is what French philosopher, and sociologist, Jacques Ellul called "Technique". In his influential work, *The Technological Society*, Ellul analyzed the pervasive influence of technology in our modern world, arguing that it goes far beyond mere tools and machinery.[61] For Ellul technique refers to the whole process of applying scientific knowledge and rational methods to achieve a specific objective. It involves the organization, efficiency, and rationalization of human activities through the use of technology. Technique shapes our behaviors, values, and ways of thinking, influencing our entire social and cultural context.

In simple terms, technique is a compulsive need to maximize efficiency, to constantly improve no matter the cost. This is in stark contrast to how medieval man saw the world; it never occurred to him to constantly improve. When medieval man manufactured a knife, he was satisfied as long as the knife did its job; he did not think to make it sharper or lighter without reason. On the other hand, modern man pushes the limits without ceasing. Our doctors pursue womb transplants and sex change surgeries, while Silicon Valley drives head-first toward automation and AI. They do this not because there is a need, but because the compulsive technique drives them. Technique will not be satisfied; it will not be stopped.

> *Technique has penetrated the deepest recesses of the human being. The machine tends not only to create a new human*

> *environment, but also to modify man's very essence. The milieu in which he lives is no longer his. He must adapt himself, as though the world were new, to a universe for which he was not created. He was made to go six kilometers an hour, and he goes a thousand. He was made to eat when he was hungry and to sleep when he was sleepy; instead, he obeys a clock. He was made to have contact with living things, and he lives in a world of stone. He was created with a certain essential unity, and he is fragmented by all the forces of the modern world.*

Ellul expressed great concern about the dehumanizing effects of technological progress, as it engulfs various aspects of life and leaves little room for genuine human agency. Technique and Technology create Frankensteinesque monsters, it permits us to divorce ourselves from human connection. This loss of connection can be seen all around us. We are no longer required to leave our homes, food, clothing cars all of it can be purchased from a couch, limited human interaction required. Our society operates like a modem where we blindly send signals back and forth. The face-to-face interchange that was once necessary for the buying and selling of goods, is no more.

The technology and technique that erode our social bonds also damage who we are. Martin Heidegger echoed these concerns about technology and its ability to alienate man from himself, from being. In *The Question Concerning Technology*, Heidegger argued that technology can alienate us from the world and ourselves.[62] He was concerned that the rapid advancement of technology would lead to a detachment from nature, a loss of connection with others, and a loss of self-understanding. Heidegger worried that technology's dominant mode of revealing could lead to a loss of our authentic relationship with Dasein (being).

> *Everywhere we remain unfree and chained to technology, whether we passionately affirm or deny it. But we are delivered over to it in the worst possible way when we regard it as something neutral; for this conception of it, to which today we particularly pay homage, makes us utterly blind to the essence of technology. -Martin Heidegger*

A quick recap of Heidegger's concept of Dasein may be necessary. Dasein is a German word that translates to "being there" or "existence." In Heidegger's philosophy, Dasein refers to human existence and the unique way in which humans experience the world. Heidegger sought to understand the fundamental nature of human existence, questioning the meaning of being and how humans relate to the world they inhabit.

Dasein is characterized by its self-awareness, the ability to question its own existence and the capacity for understanding itself and its world. Heidegger emphasized Dasein in a temporal context, existing within the past, present, and future. He also emphasized the importance of understanding

Dasein's embeddedness in the world, its practical engagements, and its relationship with other beings.

The exploration of Dasein's existence and its relationship to time, world, and Being is central to Heidegger's phenomenological inquiry in *Being and Time*.[63] By examining the nature of Dasein, Heidegger aimed to shed light on the fundamental questions of human existence.

Heidegger understood the proclivity of technology to reduce everything to resources and instrumental value, that it would obscure the deeper meaning and mystery of existence.

Heidegger's concern with technology was not a rejection of technological progress per se, but rather an invitation to critically reflect on its impact and to consider its place within the larger context of human existence. He encouraged a form of meditative thinking, where individuals contemplate their relationship with technology and its implications for authentic living (Dasein). He was optimistic be suggested that by understanding the potential hindrances, we can strive for a more balanced and mindful approach to technology's role in our lives.

The complex interplay between nature, technology, instinct, and intellect shapes our existence in profound ways. As urbanization and technology continue to dominate modern life, we are losing our authentic connection to the natural world, to Dasein, and to God. However, by understanding and reflecting on our relationship with technology, we can in our own lives search for the equilibrium of instinct and intellect, and we can regain a more meaningful and harmonious way of living.

We cannot stop the tide of technique and progress, but by embracing the essence of Dasein, our unique being-there, it may be possible that we achieve a balanced coexistence with nature and technology, allowing us to navigate the challenges of the modern world while preserving the richness of our human experience.

[48]

Techno tower Babel: Technology's Precarious Balance and the Temptation to Play God

I don't fear AI and neither should you. I'm aware of the potential dangers, but I don't believe we will ever see Skynet. For all its potential AI will be just another brick in the technological wall that is bound to collapse all around us.

While technology has done much to improve our lives. It is no secret that it has caused immeasurable damage. Technology has eroded our attention spans by giving us everything on demand. It has made us fatter by allowing us to produce enormous amounts of cheap low-quality food while reducing the need for physical activity, and it is now becoming increasingly obvious that is making us dumber. Every new technology atrophies the senses and removes us from the natural world, and man presses on ever playing God and never asking if he should only if he can.

Declining IQ Rate and the Fall of Intellectual Capacities:

In the twilight of our age, concerns have been raised regarding the declining average IQ observed in certain regions. Various factors, including environmental changes, educational deficiencies, and societal influences, have been implicated in this decline. Such diminishing intellectual capacities will lead to reduced problem-solving abilities, impaired critical thinking skills, and hindered innovation. These consequences, in turn, make sustaining and advancing complex technologies near impossible.

The push button app-driven modern technologically dependent society we live in requires an ever-increasingly complex system to maintain it. Yet that same technology has a negative effect on the overall health and intelligence of the population. Young people are losing the ability to write, read, and cook, in addition to many other necessary life skills. We have long since lost the ability to provide for ourselves, even the most basic necessities are a mystery in their origin to the younger generation. Few people today can garden, hunt, or produce clothing, they are simply reliant on the current system to provide all that they need.

The rebuttal to the above critique is something to the effect of "We don't need to do those things we have technology". While this is a fair point it rests on the presupposition that technology will be with us in perpetuity. There will be no back slide just an ever-growing technological complexity. Any basic study of history would refute this claim. Technologies have been lost and rediscovered as civilizations come and go. Nothing is permanent and to assume is in all likely hood fatal.

The history of human civilization is not the story of eternal progress but rather an ebb and flow, where civilizations rise and fall. As tiresome as the comparison of our current civilization to Rome is, it has become cliche because it fits so well. When Rome finally collapsed, Europe went into the dark ages, followed by the middle ages, then on to the Renaissance eventually soring back to the heights of Rome. So one would assume that if the United States were to collapse we would see a similar situation play out however, our collapse would be catastrophic.

When Rome finally succumbed to its fate the population that remained had the basic skills necessary to provide for themselves and their communities. The same cannot be said for a large swath of the world today. Our overreliance on technology has left us dependent, and like a junkie, the withdrawals could be fatal.

We are just now beginning to see the fruits of our labor. IQ levels have been dropping for some time and at their current trajectory the average IQ could drop as low as 85 by the end of this century. That is a number far below what is necessary to maintain such a complex network of systems that our society has become reliant on. Even if you believe that we can create automated systems capable of self-regulation those systems have to be maintained by somebody, and those people are going to become increasingly rare.

With all of this in mind, I am drawn back as I so often am to the Bible. The Tower of Babel narrative, found in the Book of Genesis, tells the tale of a civilization driven by hubris to construct a tower that would reach the heavens. Driven by their thirst for acclaim and fearful of dispersion, they sought to rival the divine. However, their arrogance and aspiration to play God invited divine intervention, resulting in the confusion of languages and the ultimate collapse of their grandiose project.

Here we emphasize the perils of human pride and the dire consequences of overstepping our boundaries without the necessary wisdom and reverence for the divine. As man uses technology to play God, God makes man too stupid to maintain his creation, and in truly divine comedic nature, it is man's tools that will drag him back to earth, technology will become incomprehensible, a foreign tongue to fresh ears.

We must embrace humility, recognize our limited nature, and relinquish the desire to ascend to the heavens without due reverence for the divine order and in the meantime prepare our children with the skills to navigate the coming storm, for those that do will be the architects of the new.

[49]

Art and Soul

[50]

Where Have All the Art Men Gone

Art is not a handicraft, it is the transmission of feeling the artist has experienced.
– Leo Tolstoy

The recent Twitter thread I posted criticizing conservatives for their lack of support for the arts sparked a flood of responses, most of which missed the point entirely. This, of course, is no surprise to anyone familiar with Twitter's dynamics. The first tweet in a thread always garners significantly more views than the last, and most users respond to the initial post without engaging with the broader argument. As a result, the nuanced point I was trying to make was lost in a sea of superficial reactions

The majority of responses I received were calls for more explicitly conservative or right-wing art. This, however, was not my argument. Art created with an overt political agenda is almost always bad art. The recent string of Disney films is evidence enough of this phenomenon. When artists prioritize political messaging over authenticity, the work loses its soul. The audience is no longer immersed in the experience; instead, they see it as either a condemnation or an endorsement of their beliefs. This serves only to alienate the audience and diminish the ability of the art to resonate on a deeper level.

What we need is not more right-wing or conservative art, but rather men with traditional or conservative ideals creating art. For generations, conservatives have discouraged their children from pursuing the arts in favor of more "practical" goals. This mindset stems from the conservative obsession with meritocracy and efficiency, which is itself rooted in a hyper-materialistic understanding of value. Figures like Dave Ramsey embody this line of thinking. Ask yourself what value Ramsey would place on the works of Herman Melville or William Faulkner, and you'll understand exactly how American conservatives view art.

This obsession with efficiency and material value has no place in the domain of art. Art's value cannot be quantified, reduced to spreadsheets, or measured by algorithmic metrics. It exists to explore the intangible, capture the complexities of the human condition, and provoke reflection and emotion. Yet, because conservatives have misunderstood this, they have systematically steered their children away from artistic pursuits. Given that political leanings are largely genetic, this has resulted in generations of right-leaning youth abandoning the arts.

The consequence of this cultural shift is that the arts have become the domain of the left. While conservative parents pushed their children toward practical skills like finance, engineering, or law, the arts gradually became saturated with individuals who naturally lean left. This created a negative feedback loop: as the arts became increasingly associated with left-wing, gay, or feminine sensibilities, conservative-leaning young men turned away in even greater numbers. The arts, in turn, became even more dominated by those with left-wing biases, further alienating conservatives. The more the arts were seen as gay the more gay the arts became.

Great art communicates universal truths about the human condition, and these truths are filtered through the political and social leanings of the artist. In the past, we had artists who were unapologetically masculine and right-wing—men like John Ford, whose films *The Searchers* and *The Quiet Man* are considered right-wing not because of any overt political messaging, but because of who John Ford was as a man. Ford's work reflects his worldview, his values, and his understanding of the human condition. Yet, men like Ford are no longer encouraged to create art. Instead, they are pushed into finance, the military, or other "practical" fields. If they do eventually turn to art, it is often late in life, after they have forfeited the years of practice and refinement necessary to hone their craft.

Historically, figures like T.S. Eliot and Flannery O'Connor produced works that were deeply rooted in their conservative values. Eliot's *The Waste Land* and O'Connor's *Wise Blood* are celebrated not for their political messaging but for exploring universal truths through a traditional or religious lens. Their work is a testament to the fact that traditionalism/ conservatism when authentically expressed, can produce some of the most enduring and profound art.

The left's monopoly on the arts has not only alienated conservatives but has also led to cultural stagnation. In their pursuit of ideological conformity contemporary artists have abandoned the exploration of universal truths in favor of shallow political pandering. The result is an artistic landscape where originality is sacrificed at the altar of progressive dogma, leaving audiences with nothing but predictable, uninspired garbage.

Art schools and universities, which serve as the gatekeepers of the cultural world, have played a significant role in sidelining conservative voices. These institutions prioritize ideological unity over artistic merit, creating an environment where conservative students feel unwelcome and ostracized. Funding organizations, too, tend to favor projects that align with progressive values, further entrenching the left's dominance in the arts.

At its core, art is about beauty—about creating something that transcends the mundane and touches the soul. The right, with its reverence for tradition, order, and aesthetic beauty, is uniquely positioned to produce art that resonates on a profound level. These ideas are timeless, they are not fleeting political agendas but are the foundation for creating works that endure and inspire.

If we ever want this to change, the right must take deliberate action. This includes supporting conservative artists through patronage and promotion, creating alternative institutions that prioritize artistic excellence over ideology, and encouraging young conservatives to pursue careers in the arts. We are uniquely positioned to begin building a cultural ecosystem that values authenticity and beauty, we can restore balance to the artistic world.

Some will argue that art has always been political, but this is a mischaracterization. While great art often reflects the artist's worldview, it does so subtly and organically, allowing the audience to draw their own conclusions. Propaganda, on the other hand, is didactic and heavy-handed, leaving no room for interpretation. Conservatives are not inherently less creative; they have simply been discouraged from participating in the arts to the detriment of both the cultural landscape and their own values.

The left is not to blame for the absence of conservative voices in the arts it is a result of their prioritization of the material over all else. Nature abhors a vacuum and the left took full advantage of the empty space and drove the right further from the arts. All the while conservatives mocked the arts behind white-collar salaries. In the end, this only helped to speed run the left's ideological dominance and the deterioration of American cultural cohesion.

We must encourage our children to pursue film, writing, and music, if not as a career at least as a serious passion project, and we must support right-leaning artists.

We can reclaim the arts.

The future of our culture depends on it.

Art is the proper task of life. – Friedrich Nietzsche

[51]

Dixie Noir: The Rebirth of Southern Gothic

Late last night, while reading over J.R. Dunmore's thoughtful exploration of Dixie Noir, I couldn't help but trace its deep roots back to the Southern Gothic tradition.[64] What Dunmore describes as a genre for "righteous outlaws" strikes me as an evolution of the haunted South we know from Faulkner and O'Connor, reframed for a modern audience steeped in nihilism and moral ambiguity. It's Noir that is rooted, defiant, and unapologetically Southern.

What defines Dixie Noir isn't just its Southern setting or its gritty aesthetic—though the brooding heat, slow Southern drawls, and swamp-bound corpses certainly help. It's a genre that speaks directly to the soul of the Southern ethos, rejecting the clinical detachment of traditional Noir in favor of something far more visceral. In the South, justice has always been personal. The concept of "self-help" that Dunmore describes—the willingness to take justice into one's own hands—isn't just a plot device; it's a way of life.

This is the fundamental break between the stoic detectives of Raymond Chandler's world and the protagonists of Dixie Noir. The hard-boiled detective is a man trapped within a crumbling system, resigned to play by the rules even when those rules betray him. The Dixie Noir protagonist, by contrast, sees the system for what it is—a façade—and steps outside it without hesitation. To him, loyalty, justice, and family matter more than laws ever could. Both protagonists are acutely aware of the system's corruption. For the traditional Noir detective, this corruption is a tragic byproduct of poor governance. For the Southern Noir hero, it's simply the way things are. For the Northerner, Tammany Hall was a tragedy; for the Southerner, it's just politics as usual.

And here is where Dixie Noir sets itself apart. It rejects the cynicism and fatalism of traditional Noir. Instead, it clings tightly to a sense of hope—not in institutions, but in individuals. Where traditional Noir might leave its heroes broken or dead, Dixie Noir allows them to emerge transformed. Scarred, yes. Haunted, certainly. But alive, and all the better for the fight. If traditional Noir is the story of a man struggling to survive within a broken system, Dixie Noir is the story of a man who decides to break the system himself. It's a genre for those who refuse to go quietly into the night.

As Dunmore points out Dixie Noir carves has its own aesthetic identity. It trades the dark, seedy underbelly of Northern cities for the suffocating humidity of the Gulf Coast, the rhythmic tap of rain on tin roofs, and the shadowed secrets of small towns tangled in kudzu and Spanish moss. It offers readers an invitation to a world where beauty and violence are forever intertwined, where dirt roads wind through landscapes as haunted as the histories of the characters who traverse them.

But its most important distinction lies in its relationship with the past. Dixie Noir inherits from its Southern Gothic roots a kind of spiritual PTSD that transcends generations, manifesting in the form of magical realism. This separates it from its more grounded, urban-centered Noir counterpart and gives it a sense of mystery and weight that feels uniquely Southern.

The South has always been a place where the line between the natural and the supernatural blurs. It is a land where the veil between the spiritual and temporal is disturbingly thin, where ghosts linger on front porches, family curses twist fate, and the land itself pulses with the memory of what once was. In Dixie Noir, this undercurrent of the uncanny doesn't just add atmosphere, it actively shapes the narrative. It hangs heavy over its characters, influencing them in ways both subtle and explicit, without an attempt at rationalization.

In the South, the land breathes with a life of its own, whispering the secrets of the past to those willing to listen. Storms don't merely rage—they become omens, manifestations of wrath or redemption. And the characters, even the most pragmatic among them, move through a world where signs and superstitions carry as much weight as fingerprints and shell casings. This haunting spirituality defines the genre, rooting the fight for justice in a landscape where the spiritual and the corporeal are irrevocably intertwined.

[52]

In the Shadows of Faith: The Noir Approach to Christian Narratives

Christian Fiction is a genre that I am well acquainted with. Growing up in an Evangelical environment, I was bombarded with attempts to supplement popular media with Christian alternatives. At its best, this came in the form of talking vegetables; at its worst, there was Bibleman. The older I got, the further from reality Christian media seemed to be. Life became more complicated, morality grayed, and the WWJD bracelets disappeared.

Despite the harsh reality of life, the vast majority of Christian media remained dominated by happy-go-lucky feel-good dramas, where the central message is some variation of "Pray hard, and God will solve all your problems." To be fair, the intentions are good, and I cannot fault the filmmakers for trying to craft captivating storylines while being handcuffed by the limitations of Mega Church Christianity. It is difficult to explore the complexities of human nature and the darker side of mankind when your philosophy is dominated by emotionalism.

The result is that when people hear a book or a film described as Christian, they roll their eyes and assume it will be intellectually shallow, some combination of the 700 Club and Hallmark. As an amateur writer, I found myself struggling to conceptualize what a compelling narrative with Christian themes would look like. I found the answer to the question in my love of Noir.

Noir is a particular subgenre of crime fiction that deals with the darker side of humanity. Andrew Pepper, in an essay published in The Cambridge Companion to American Crime Fiction, described Noir as a genre that deals with "the corrosive effects of money, the meaninglessness, and absurdity of existence, anxieties about masculinity and the bureaucratization of public life, a fascination with the grotesque, and a flirtation with, and rejection of, Freudian Psychoanalysis." It is a genre that looks at humanity in the most Christian of terms, that of man as a fallen and corrupted being incapable of self-salvation.

In these dark and sordid tales lies the key to crafting compelling Christian narratives. What is a more powerful example of the power of Christ than the redeeming of those labeled irredeemable?

The Noir protagonist is a man forced to navigate a world solid with corruption, a world of vice and sin where nothing seems capable of escaping the darkness that haunts mankind. He is often a broken man, haunted by his own sin and selfishly motivated by the same vice that drives his enemies. He is nearly indistinguishable in motivation or morality from the antagonist that he faces. To put it simply, he is human.

Because of this humanity, his salvation can only be obtained through self-sacrifice. He must deny himself and all that he desires, often giving his own life for those who may very well squander the second chance he affords them. In other words, he must be Christlike.

The crucial insight isn't merely that Noir is the genre for telling Christian stories, but rather that to craft narratives that explore and effectively communicate Christian themes, we must confront humanity in its raw, unfiltered state—with all the suffering and pain inherent in a fallen world. It demands a realization that it is through the most unlikely characters that Christ reveals Himself. If the goal is to tell Christian stories authentically, one must intimately understand the darker facets of humanity, for it is in the shadows that the light shines most brilliantly

[53]

From Dystopia to Divine: Christian Symbolism in Gene Wolfe's Book of the New Sun

Within the tapestry of speculative fiction, where imagination weaves the fabric of worlds, Gene Wolfe's *The Book of the New Sun*[65] stands as a masterpiece intricately entwined with threads of Christian allegory. Spanning the quartet of novels—namely, "The Shadow of the Torturer," "The Claw of the Conciliator," "The Sword of the Lictor," and "The Citadel of the Autarch"—this opus is more than a mere saga of dystopian fiction. It emerges as a profound exploration of faith, redemption, and the transformative power of Christian symbolism.

As the sun's luminance wanes, casting a feeble glow upon a world grappling with scarcity and decay, a central promise—the advent of a "New Sun"—rises like a beacon of spiritual renewal. This promise echoes the Christian belief in resurrection and salvation, mirroring the anticipation of Christ's second coming. Just as the faithful await the ultimate renewal of the world, Wolfe's characters yearn for a radiant dawn that transcends the limitations of mortality.

At the heart of this odyssey stands Severian, whose evolution from a humble apprentice torturer to the mantle of the Conciliator mirrors the Christian journey of spiritual growth and redemption. Severian's path echoes the archetypal hero's quest—a transformative expedition that demands trials, sacrifices, and the audacity to confront the unknown. Through Severian's ordeals, the narrative encapsulates the inherent human desire for purpose, enlightenment, and transcendence.

The literary tableau becomes a canvas for a captivating interplay between philosophy and fiction. Severian's contemplations on time, morality, and the intricate interplay between human agency and cosmic destiny resonate with the inquiries of theologians and philosophers throughout history. In an inspired fusion of prose and faith, Wolfe compels readers to explore profound philosophical questions, akin to the journey of faith that propels individuals to probe the mysteries of existence.

Religious allusions and symbolism infuse the narrative with layers of meaning, inviting readers to plumb the depths of spiritual truth. The enigmatic term "diabolical eucharist" resonates with the sacrament of the Eucharist in the Catholic tradition, exemplifying the interplay between the temporal and the divine. This infusion of Christian elements forms a profound synergy between the narrative's fiction and the author's own faith, infusing the tale with a resonance that echoes through the corridors of eternity.

The figure of the Conciliator, a Christ-like presence that graces the narrative, becomes a fulcrum around which the story pivots. Analogous to Christ's redemptive work, the Conciliator embodies themes of sacrifice, healing, and the ultimate triumph of good over evil. Mirroring Christ's miracles, the Conciliator employs the Claw of the Conciliator to perform wonders, echoing the miracles attributed to Christ and magnifying the spiritual dimension of the narrative.

Resurrection, a recurring motif, weaves its way through the narrative tapestry. Characters experience a form of resurrection that underscores the cyclical nature of life and death—a theme central to Christian theology. This motif captures the hope of resurrection embedded in Christianity, where death is not an end, but a passage to new life. Wolfe's incorporation of this theme invites readers to reflect upon the transformative and eternal nature of the soul.

The series embodies the notion that life itself is an odyssey—a ceaseless journey of faith, discovery, and redemption. Severian's voyage, fraught with moral dilemmas and ethical quandaries, encapsulates the essence of human existence. His contemplation of mercy, justice, and his role within a morally ambiguous world mirrors the broader struggle of individuals navigating their own moral landscapes. The narrative, thus, becomes a mirror reflecting the readers' own ethical journey and prompting contemplation of faith.

Ultimately, "The Book of the New Sun" emerges as a literary triumph—an intricate fusion of philosophy, faith, and storytelling. Its pages invite readers to wrestle with the very fabric of existence, to grapple with profound inquiries, and to embark on a spiritual odyssey alongside its characters. The journey of faith is not linear; it mirrors the cyclical passage from darkness to light, akin to the resurrection and renewal embedded within Christian belief.

Gene Wolfe's magnum opus stands as a testament to the enduring potency of Christian allegory in literature. Through layers of narrative depth, intricate character arcs, and profound philosophical exploration, "The Book of the New Sun" weaves a narrative tapestry that resonates on a deeply spiritual level. As readers traverse its labyrinthine passages, they journey through their own spiritual landscapes, drawn into the eternal quest for redemption, enlightenment, and an ultimate union with the divine.

[54]

On Patrons and Patronage

In my recent article, *Where Have All the Art Men Gone,* I critiqued the lack of right-leaning or conservative representation in the arts. I argued that the emphasis on financial and skill-based value created a situation in which right-leaning individuals did not pursue the arts, allowing the field to be completely overtaken by the left. This resulted in a negative feedback loop: as the arts became increasingly coded as left-wing, conservatives disengaged even further. While I still stand by that assessment, another, perhaps even more crucial, factor is at play—patronage.

Throughout history, the vast majority of great artists were funded by patrons. Often, these patrons were wealthy individuals who subsidized art they deemed valuable. However, it was not just private wealth that funded the arts; the government also played a considerable role.

In fact, government-supported art has been one of the most important factors in the proliferation of artistic expression and the molding of taste. For artists to have the time and freedom to create great works, someone has to foot the bill. If it is not a patron or the government, then the artists must support themselves, and this leaves little time for creative pursuits.

Many conservatives recoil at the idea of state-funded art, dismissing it as propaganda or a restriction on free speech. However, state-sponsored art has always existed. If you grew up during the GWOT era, you were inundated with state-run propaganda. Every time you turned on the TV to watch a football game and saw jets flying overhead, a color guard marching onto the field, and a massive flag unfurled at the 50-yard line, you were witnessing a state-funded propaganda campaign.

These were not organic patriotic displays driven by the NFL's love of country—they were carefully crafted wartime propaganda paid for with tax dollars. This influence extended beyond sports. Hollywood has been one of the greatest military recruiting tools as well. The Pentagon has influenced hundreds of films and TV shows, including *Top Gun*, *Transformers*, and *Iron Man*. All of this is made possible through the Department of Defense Entertainment Media Office, which provides military resources to filmmakers in exchange for script revisions that portray the military in a positive light.

None of this is new. The Works Progress Administration (WPA) during the New Deal funded thousands of artists, writers, and performers in the 1930s. Both Stan Lee and Dr. Seuss got their start creating propaganda posters for the U.S. military during World War II. The vast majority of World War II films released in the decade following the war were funded by the U.S. government. This is not to say that figures like John Ford or John Wayne were not patriotic, but their artistic expressions of patriotism were financially supported by the state.

It is a tale as old as art itself. The Medici family in Renaissance Italy funded many great artists, including Michelangelo and Leonardo da Vinci. Meanwhile, the French Académie des Beaux-Arts heavily state-supported and shaped European art for centuries. The point is explicit: if the right wants to influence culture, they must invest in the arts. This requires not only individuals willing to pursue artistic endeavors but also financial backers willing to fund them.

It is an uncomfortable discussion. As a writer, the last thing I want to consider is having my work funded by the government, an organization, or a politically motivated wealthy patron. But the reality remains—if you want your art to be impactful or lucrative, someone has to finance it.

Nowhere is this more evident than in the publishing industry. Recent lawsuits have revealed that major publishing companies remain afloat thanks to the revenue generated by a handful of perennial bestsellers. They publish a slew of mediocre books, but their financial stability relies on continually reprinting popular works like *Dune* and *The Lord of the Rings*. Additionally, they profit from the fact that every high school in the country is required to purchase copies of *To Kill a Mockingbird* and *The Great Gatsby* every few years.

This type of funding not only sustains publishing companies but also ensures that students are exposed to the literature favored by those in power. This is not a neutral process. Many novels that we deem classics were given that status through schools due to government or institutional decisions rather than purely on literary merit.

One should not assume that federal or state education departments objectively decided that *The Great Gatsby* or *Of Mice and Men* are the best books for high school curricula. To be sure, they are great novels, but their selection is deliberate. That same government apparatus could just as easily mandate that every eighth grader read *The Screwtape Letters* or *Mere Christianity*, but it does not—and that is a conscious decision. We may not like it but this state funding is a powerful form of patronage.

Imagine the impact if the powers that be decided that every high school civics class had to read *Unqualified Reservations*, or if Nick Land's work were part of a mandatory political science curriculum. I do not like the idea of artistic propaganda any more than anyone else—it feels dishonest, even dirty, but it works.

Studies show that exposure to certain books, films, or art can shift political opinions over time. The Frankfurt School and cultural Marxist theories emphasize how left-leaning academics have and do shape artistic and literary discourse. The reality is that art is one of the most powerful tools for communicating ideas, and someone is always deciding what people are exposed to.

And this is another uncomfortable truth: none of us decide what we like in a vacuum. If you developed a love for Southern literature, it is because someone pointed you toward Faulkner or Walker Percy. Again, this is not to say they are not great writers, but rather that your choices were, in part, shaped for you. Look at the answers people give when asked about the greatest films of all time. Over and over you will see people list *The Godfather*, *Apocalypse Now*, or *Citizen Kane*, yet how many of those people have actually watched those films? I would bet that most people who name those movies have not seen them—they have been convinced that those are the films you are supposed to name to sound cultured.

The reality is that someone has to be the tastemaker, and that role falls to the patron. The patron decides which works of art reach the public. The artist is merely the vessel for transmitting ideas, while the patron determines which ideas are pushed when, and how.

If we want a right-leaning artistic movement, we need money—plain and simple. That is the uncomfortable truth. Where do we go from here? Perhaps that is a topic for another essay. But my early thoughts are these: we must find wealthy, financially independent traditional-minded individuals and convince them that funding the arts has value. This will be a difficult task because, as I mentioned earlier, conservatives—especially the wealthy—tend to dismiss the arts as superfluous and left-coded. This perception will only change when they realize that funding a writer to create a great screenplay, produce a film, or develop a video game is just as valuable as buying a politician. They need to see that the artist is the lobbyist for culture.

It will be a long road, and the return on investment is not immediate—it is slow. But to truly change the culture, you need both immediate and long-term strategies. Reshaping institutions is one part of the equation, but so is funding and producing new art.

Consider the long-term consequences of establishing a system in which every student must read *The Abolition of Man* or Alexis de Tocqueville's works. Doing so would shape generations of right-wing thought and plant ideological seeds that could challenge liberalism.

The arts are worth funding. They are greater than the sum of their parts.

[55]

The Secret of TeenagerdomSlopification vs Infantilization

> *The tragedy of modern man is not that he knows less and less about the meaning of his own life, but that it bothers him less and less. — Václav Havel*

Reading through, Dave Greene's[66] and Alexandru Constantin's[67] recent back-and-forth about the "slopification" versus infantilization of media debate has been quite interesting. Both men point to something fundamentally wrong with our perception of modern media—whether it's the attempt to find meaning in content meant for children or the obvious degradation in quality. While both Dave and Constantin make valid points, their assessment is missing a crucial factor: the phenomenon of the aging teenager.

The teenager is an artificial creation of modernity. Before the 1950s, people transitioned directly from childhood to adolescence to adulthood. However, as consumerist culture took hold, it recognized the untapped monetary potential of youth. For the first time in history, society had an abundance of adolescents with expendable income, leading to the birth of an entire media ecosystem designed to market and sell music, movies, and television to them. This era saw the rise of artists like Elvis and Buddy Holly, specifically targeted at this new demographic, and with it came the term "teenager."

The difference between an adolescent and a teenager is not just semantic but one of purpose and function. Adolescents—no longer children—were traditionally prepared for adulthood. They transitioned from childhood into roles of increasing responsibility, so that by 18, they were getting married and having children by their early 20s.

In contrast, the teenager represents a form of arrested development. Rather than being prepared for adulthood, teenagers were freed from the expectation of responsibility and instead encouraged to focus on self-discovery and personal identity. In essence, the teenager is an extension of childhood.

The Greatest Generation was the first generation to experience this phenomenon. Yet it is the Boomers who grew up with the teenager as a social norm and this extended adolescence manifested in the cultural revolution of the 1960s. However, they still carried traces of older adolescent culture and were never fully immersed in the cult of the teenager. That transformation would reach its full potential with their children, the Millennials.

From the Boomers onward, an entire media industry emerged to capitalize on youth culture. The financial incentives were too great to ignore, and soon even childhood itself was monetized. The first generation creating media for children had been raised in an adolescent culture, so they still infused their work with moral and ethical lessons necessary for adulthood.

Films like *Watership Down* and *The Secret of NIMH* exemplify this mindset. Though targeted at children, they contain deep, meaningful lessons about human nature, life, and responsibility—essentially adult stories packaged for younger audiences. These stand in stark contrast to today's children's media, a shift driven by the gradual replacement of those with adolescence residue by those baptized in teenagerdom. With each passing generation, arrested development has only intensified.

Despite pioneering teenagerdom, Boomers were still forced to grow up at a relatively normal pace. They got married in their late teens, had children in their early 20s, and started careers. Generation X extended this timeline into their late 20s, with college serving as an extension of youthful self-discovery. By the time Millennials came of age, youth had been prolonged well into their early 30s.

I am in the minority among my generation—at 37, I am married with children, the eldest of whom is approaching 13. Most of my peers, however, are in their mid-30s, unmarried, and childless. They have not grown up; they still party and live attachemntless, and outside of their careers, they behave much as they did as teenagers—only with more money.

Boomers let go of childish things early, Gen X a little later, and Millennials not at all. The result? We now have media produced by adults who think and act like teenagers, consumed by adults who never grew up. They seek adult themes in the toys they never put away.

When Dave sees "slop," in today's media it's because he is looking for meaning in content made for adults by emotionally stunted adults. This stands in stark contrast to the media of our youth, which still carried the expectation of adolescent growth. Therefore, he is correct to call it what it is... slop. By that same token, Constantin is also correct when he says we are searching for value in what is, at its core, a child's toy. However, that toy has also degraded in quality to what Dave rightly calls "slopificaiton."

Ultimately, this debate is not just about media but about the cultural consequences of prolonged adolescence. As each generation extends youth further into adulthood, the media they consume reflects that stagnation. What we see today is not just a decline in quality but a fundamental shift in purpose—stories once meant to prepare the young for adulthood are now created by and for those who refuse to grow up. In the end, both Dave and Constantin are right, but their perspectives are two sides of the same coin: a culture that refuses to put away childish things and no longer understands how to make them meaningful.

[56]

Sometimes Nothin' Can Be a Real Cool Hand

Now just where am I supposed to fit in? Old Man, I gotta tell You. I started out pretty strong and fast. But it's beginning to get to me. When does it end? What do You got in mind for me? What do I do now? – Luke Jackson, Cool Hand Luke

I've lost count of how many times I've watched Cool Hand Luke. For as far back as memory serves, it's been my cinematic favorite, featuring great performances by Paul Newman and George Kennedy, along with some of the most memorable lines in the history of cinema. It is a film that simultaneously speaks to the existential struggle of the authentic self, manifesting in a world from which it is rejected while also being a deeply Christian film.

For the uninitiated, Cool Hand Luke narrates the

story of Luke Jackson, a man seemingly incapable of adapting to the world around him. The film opens with Luke drunkenly cutting the heads off parking meters with a pipe cutter. Arrested for this act of vandalism, he's sentenced to two years of hard time. Upon arriving at the prison, he becomes just another new inmate, facing hostility from the veteran criminals he's housed with. Initially, his rebellious nature clashes with his fellow convicts, but over time, his resilience, honesty, and refusal to give up earn their respect. Unable to cope with captivity, Luke manages multiple escapes, becoming a lackey for the guards after they try to break him and receiving the cold shoulder from other inmates once he no longer represents freedom of spirit to them. But, of course, Luke's spirit can never be chained, leading to one last escape attempt that results in his final martyrdom.

While Luke is undoubtedly an allegorical Christ-like figure (a topic I'll delve into later), he also embodies a natural contrarian. Watching the film, one gets the sense that Luke can't help trying to escape any more than a cat can help chasing mice—it's inherent to his nature. The rest of the world can put on a mask, genuflect to authorities, but for Luke, it seems impossible.

This inability to conform is something Luke is acutely aware of, portrayed vividly in scenes where he prays. He lashes out at God, questioning why he was made this way.

Anybody here? Hey, Old Man. You home tonight? Can You spare a minute. It's about time we had a little talk. I know I'm a pretty evil fellow... killed people in the war and got drunk... and chewed up municipal property and the like. I know I got no call to ask for much... but even so, You've got to admit You ain't dealt me no cards in a long time. It's beginning to look like You got things fixed so I can't never win out. Inside, outside, all of them... rules and regulations and bosses. You made me like I am. Now just where am I supposed to fit in? Old Man, I gotta tell You. I started out pretty strong and fast. But it's beginning to get to me. When does it end? What do You got in mind for me? What do I do now? Right. All right."
– Luke Jackson

His contrarian nature is almost a curse, an original sin, something he doesn't desire but carries like a burden. Again, he lashes out at God, questioning why he was made this way.

One could argue that Luke is a rebel for the sake of rebellion, and perhaps that's true; the film overtly portrays the externalism of the late 1960s. I find it more likely that Luke is simply a man who cannot live under an authority he deems illegitimate or evil. When he arrives at the prison, the other inmates, by and large, follow orders and obey the rules to avoid the warden's wrath. Luke can't comply. He pushes back, not in a violently aggressive way, but through nonviolent means of protest, making a run for it whenever possible.

In many ways, Luke stands for many of us on the Dissident Right. Like Luke, we live under a regime we perceive as illegitimate or evil, a sentiment shared by those around us. Yet, we find ourselves pushing back almost instinctively, unable to sit idly by.

Most people are content to toil anonymously under the regime's thumb, as long as they get what they need, willing to go along to get along. It's an option offered to all of us, yet we reject comfort, opting to post anonymously on Twitter, write essays on Substack, and create videos critiquing those who rule over us. We undertake these actions at great risk, endangering our jobs, livelihoods, families, and friends. Why?

Because we must. It's something inside us that won't allow us to stand by. In another time, we might have been inclined to greatness. We are men who feel the need to do something. Unlike Luke, we benefit from the Internet, flawed as it may be, allowing us to connect; we're not alone.

This connection provides a strength Luke never had. He experienced a constant state of existential crisis because he felt alone in the world. He couldn't help himself, and when asked why he did what he did, he couldn't find an answer.

We don't face that problem; we have each other. We can reach out, connect with others whose authentic selves are in constant combat with the world. There's a little bit of Luke in all of us; that's why we're here, why we do what we do. And we must accept that it is inevitable.

I often wonder, "Why can't I sit back and watch sports or engage in other activities and ignore what's happening around me? Why can't I be placated by the bread and circuses that satisfy so many others?" I think the answer is the same for me as it is for Luke, "I guess I'm pretty tough to deal with... A hard case... I guess I gotta find my own way." Perhaps it's just delusions of grandeur, but I like to think that all of us are made for something better; that's why we're here. We'd rather risk everything than sit in comfortable silence; we'd rather find our own way.

[57]

Imperium: Yockey's Unyielding Cycle of Destiny

We have been born into a certain Culture, at a certain phase of its organic development, we have certain gifts. These condition the earthly task which we must perform. The metaphysical task is beyond any conditioning, for it would have been the same in any age anywhere. The earthly task is merely the form of the higher task, its organic vehicle.

-Francis Parker Yockey

There's a haunting inevitability in the fate of civilizations, a rhythm as old as time, whispered by the winds that sweep across the ruins of forgotten empires. This lament of civilizations—birth, glory, decay, and death—is the unyielding cycle that Francis Parker Yockey devoted his life to understanding. To Yockey, civilizations were not merely collections of people bound by geography or politics; they were living, breathing entities, with souls as real as the human heart. And like all living things, they were subject to the inexorable laws of life and death.

In the dim twilight of the 20th century, Yockey emerged as a prophet of decline, his voice steeped in the despair of a man who saw the vitality of his civilization slipping away. His magnum opus, *Imperium: The Philosophy of History and Politics,* is not just a book but a mournful meditation on the cyclical nature of history, influenced by the grand theorist of cyclical history, Oswald Spengler. Yet, Yockey did not merely echo Spengler; he expanded upon the themes of cultural pessimism, infusing them with a sharp critique of the forces he believed were hastening the West's decline: materialism, rationalism, and the erosion of racial and cultural identity.

The Lifecycle of Civilizations

History is the record of fulfilled destinies— of Cultures, nations, religions, philosophies, sciences, mathematics, art forms, great men. -Francis Parker Yockey

Yockey's vision of history is not one of linear progress, nor perpetual advancement. Instead, it is a gloomy dance with death, a pattern etched in the annals of time. Civilizations, according to Yockey, are like the great oak trees of old forests—they rise from humble beginnings, grow strong and tall, and inevitably, they begin to rot from within, their roots weakened, until one day they fall, returning to the earth from which they came.

This cyclical view, inherited from Spengler, frames history as the story of rise and fall, of civilizations born in the fire of creativity, reaching a zenith of cultural and political power, only to be consumed by the very success that once sustained them. Yockey divides the lifecycle of a civilization into distinct stages, each marked by its own characteristics, each a step toward the inevitable decline.

Birth is where it all begins—where a new culture emerges, distinct and vibrant, driven by a unique spirit. This spirit, or *Cultural Vitalism*, is the lifeblood of the civilization, the essence that gives it form and purpose. It's in this stage that civilizations are at their most creative, their most dynamic, driven by a sense of destiny, a mission to carve out a place in the world.

But the seeds of decay are sown in the very soil that gives rise to the civilization. As it **grows**, expanding its influence, building grand cities, and establishing powerful institutions, the culture begins to fossilize. The **maturity** of a civilization is both its peak and the beginning of its end. It is during this time that the civilization's greatest achievements are realized—monuments are built, arts flourish, and philosophy reaches its zenith. But this is also when the civilization starts to turn inward, focusing on maintaining its glory rather than expanding it, and the once-vibrant culture begins to petrify.

Then comes the decline, the slow, agonizing process of a civilization losing its vitality. The spirit that once drove it to greatness fades, replaced by a hollow focus on material wealth and power. Institutions become rigid, innovation wanes, and society becomes more concerned with preserving the status quo than with pursuing new ideas or goals. This is the stage where Yockey sees Western civilization today—a once-great culture, now more concerned with maintaining its wealth and power than with the creative spirit that made it great in the first place.

Finally, there is death—the point at which the civilization can no longer sustain itself. It may be conquered by a more vibrant culture, or it may simply collapse under the weight of its own decadence. The civilization's spirit, its *Cultural Vitalism*, is exhausted, leaving behind only ruins and memories.

Yockey's view of civilizations as living organisms, subject to the same laws of life and death as any other living thing, is a profound and deeply pessimistic vision. It is a view that sees decline not as an anomaly, but as the natural and inevitable outcome of success. For Yockey, there is no escaping the cycle—no civilization, no matter how great, can escape the fate that awaits it.

The Soul of a Civilization

Since a Culture is organic, it has an individuality, and a soul. Thus it cannot be influenced in its depths from any outside force whatever. It has a destiny, like all organisms... Because it has a soul, all of its manifestations will be impressed by the same spiritual stamp, just as each man's life is the creation of his own individuality. -Francis Parker Yockey

At the heart of Yockey's philosophy is the idea of *Cultural Vitalism*—the soul of a civilization, the essence that drives its development and gives it purpose. This concept, borrowed from Spengler but refined by Yockey, is the key to understanding the rise and fall of civilizations.

Cultural Vitalism is not something that can be seen or measured; it is an intangible force, a spirit that infuses a civilization with life. It is the source of a civilization's creativity, its art, its philosophy, its very identity. Without it, a civilization is nothing more than a collection of people and buildings—alive in name only.

In the early stages of a civilization, this vital force is at its strongest. It is the driving energy that propels the civilization forward, that inspires its people to create, to build, to explore. It is this spirit that gives a civilization its unique character, its sense of purpose, and its place in the world.

As a civilization grows, its *Cultural Vitalism* drives it

to achieve greatness. This is the period of expansion, of conquest, of cultural flourishing. The civilization's art and philosophy reach new heights, its political institutions solidify, and its influence spreads across the world. This is the civilization at its most vibrant, its most alive.

But with maturity comes complacency. As the civilization reaches its peak, its *Cultural Vitalism* begins to wane. The focus shifts from creation to preservation, from innovation to maintaining the status quo. The once-vibrant culture begins to ossify, its creative energies dissipating. The civilization becomes more concerned with material wealth and power than with the spirit that once drove it forward.

This decline in *Cultural Vitalism* is the beginning of the end. As the civilization loses its creative energy, it becomes vulnerable to decay and collapse. The institutions that once held it together become rigid and bureaucratic, unable to adapt to new challenges.

In the end, the *Cultural Vitalism* that once defined the civilization is exhausted, leaving behind only a hollow shell. The civilization may continue to exist in name, but its spirit is gone. What remains is a society that is stagnant, devoid of creativity, and ultimately, doomed to collapse.

Yockey's idea of *Cultural Vitalism* is a powerful concept. It is a way of understanding the rise and fall of civilizations not just as a series of events, but as a process driven by the very soul of the civilization itself. It is a view that sees culture as the essence of a civilization, the force that gives it life, and the loss of that force as the cause of its decline.

Materialism and Rationalism

Materialists have never been the respecters of facts—whatever was not measurable by their ruler did not exist. -Francis Parker Yockey

In Yockey's view, the decline of Western civilization is not just a result of the natural cycle of history, but of specific forces that have eroded its *Cultural Vitalism*. Chief among these are materialism and rationalism—ideologies that Yockey believed had sapped the West of its spiritual and cultural energy, leaving it vulnerable to decay.

Materialism, in Yockey's eyes, is the obsession with wealth and power, the focus on material success at the expense of higher values. It is a force that reduces everything to its economic value, that measures success in terms of money and possessions rather than in terms of cultural and spiritual achievements. Yockey saw materialism as a corrosive force, one that had led the West away from its cultural roots and toward a shallow, empty existence.

Rationalism, closely related to materialism, is the belief that reason and logic are the only valid ways of understanding the world. Yockey saw rationalism as the enemy of tradition, religion, and culture—forces that he believed were essential to maintaining the

Cultural Vitalism of a civilization. Rationalism, in Yockey's view, stripped the West of its spiritual dimension, reducing culture to a mere intellectual exercise, devoid of deeper meaning.

Together, materialism and rationalism form the twin pillars of what Yockey saw as the West's decline. They are the ideologies that have led the West to focus on material success and technological progress at the expense of its cultural and spiritual values. They are the forces that have eroded the *Cultural Vitalism* of the West, leaving it vulnerable to decline and collapse.

Yockey's critique of materialism and rationalism is a lament for the lost spirit of the West. It is a call to return to the higher values that once defined Western civilization—values of creativity, spirituality, and cultural identity. Yockey believed that only by rejecting materialism and rationalism could the West hope to revive its *Cultural Vitalism* and stave off its inevitable decline.

Cultural and Racial Identity

For Yockey, the decline of Western civilization is also closely tied to the erosion of its cultural and racial identity. He believed that a strong and vibrant civilization could only be sustained in a society where there was a high degree of cultural and racial homogeneity. The mixing of different cultures and races within a single society, Yockey argued, leads to cultural dilution and the weakening of the *Cultural Vitalism* that is necessary for a civilization's survival.

Cultural identity, for Yockey, is the essence of a civilization—the unique set of values, traditions, and beliefs that define it. When this identity is diluted, the civilization loses its sense of purpose, its *Cultural Vitalism* begins to fade, and the society becomes vulnerable to decline.

Racial identity, in Yockey's view, is equally important. He believed that race was a fundamental component of a civilization's identity and that the preservation of racial purity was essential to maintaining the cultural and spiritual vitality of the society. Yockey argued that the decline of the West was partly due to the mixing of races, which he saw as leading to the degeneration of the civilization's *Cultural Vitalism*.

These views on cultural and racial identity are among the most controversial aspects of Yockey's thought. They have been widely criticized for their association with far-right ideologies, however, this is often misunderstood due to a simplistic view of race.

In Yockey's vision, race is more than a mere biological marker; it is the spiritual essence of a people, the invisible thread that binds them to their ancestors and their cultural destiny. For Yockey, race transcends the physical, embodying the collective soul of a civilization, shaping its art, its values, its very way of being. It is not the color of one's skin or the shape of one's features that defines race, but the shared spirit, the common destiny that courses through the veins of a people, giving life to their culture and purpose to their existence. For Yockey, anyone can become racially Western, while it may be harder for some groups than others, if an individual repudiates their prior cultural ties and embraces the West wholeheartedly they can become Western.

To Yockey, the erosion of racial identity is not just a loss of physical homogeneity but a spiritual death, a severing of the connection to the vital force that sustains a civilization. Without this spiritual race, a people lose their sense of self, their culture withers, and their civilization inevitably falls into decline.

Liberalism and Democracy

Thus the whole liberal-democratic ideology, with its individualism that is a mere negation of everything superpersonal its happiness ideal that encourages ever weakness and self-indulgence, its erotomania which distorts the whole sexual life into a barren disease of the will, its tolerance with seeks to break down the cohesion of the race by denying its existence, its materialism which denies all spiritual values, all higher significance of human life, its pacifism which values weakness above virility, its ideal of mediocrity by which it opposes every creative man and the idea he represents in history its could of the proletarian as the highest element its total renunciation of the soul of man— is the greatest enemy."

-Francis Parker Yockey

Yockey's critique of the West extends to its political systems as well. He was a vehement critic of liberalism and democracy, which he believed were incompatible with the preservation of a strong and vibrant civilization. In Yockey's view, these systems promoted individualism, materialism, and egalitarianism—all of which he saw as contributing to the decline of Western civilization.

Liberalism, for Yockey, is the ideology of individual rights and freedoms. It is a system that prioritizes the needs and desires of the individual over the collective good, leading to a society that is fragmented and lacking in cultural cohesion. Yockey argued that liberalism's emphasis on equality and tolerance led to the erosion of traditional cultural values and the weakening of the *Cultural Vitalism* necessary for the civilization's survival.

Democracy, in Yockey's view, is a flawed system of government that promotes mediocrity and the rule of the masses. He believed that democracy led to the empowerment of the "lowest common denominator" in society, undermining the authority of the cultural elite who were responsible for preserving and advancing the civilization's *Cultural Vitalism*. Yockey saw democracy as a symptom of the West's decline—a system that had led to the erosion of cultural and spiritual values and the rise of materialism and rationalism.

For Yockey, the failures of liberalism and democracy were not just political problems but cultural ones. He believed that these systems were incompatible with the preservation of a strong and vibrant civilization and that they had contributed to the decline of the West. Yockey argued that only by rejecting liberalism and democracy could the West hope to revive its *Cultural Vitalism* and restore its cultural and spiritual identity.

The Vision of Imperium: A Unified Europe

Nor is the Idea of Imperium to be confused with any stupid rationalistic doctrine or system, any cowardly millennium.
-Francis Parker Yockey

Yockey's vision for the future of Western civilization was both authoritarian and pan-European. He believed that the only way to revive the West's *Cultural Vitalism* and resist its decline was to establish a unified European empire—a concept he called *Imperium*. This *Imperium* would transcend individual nation-states, uniting the diverse nations of Europe under a single cultural and political authority.

Yockey's *Imperium* was not just a political entity but a cultural and spiritual one. He believed that only through a unified Europe could the West hope to preserve its cultural identity and resist the forces of decline. The *Imperium* would be led by a cultural elite—individuals who were deeply connected to the civilization's cultural and spiritual values. This elite would guide the civilization towards a renewal of its

Cultural Vitalism, working to preserve and advance its cultural achievements.

Yockey's vision of *Imperium* was also pan-European in scope. He believed that the nation-state system, with its emphasis on national sovereignty and individualism, was incompatible with the preservation of Western civilization. Instead, Yockey advocated for a united Europe, where the various nations would be subsumed into a single cultural and political entity. This, he argued, was necessary to resist the external pressures of rising non-Western civilizations and to promote the cultural and spiritual rejuvenation of the West.

The idea of the *Imperium* is central to Yockey's thought. It is his answer to the decline of Western civilization—a vision of a future where the West can resist the forces of decay and restore its *Cultural Vitalism*. For Yockey, *Imperium* was not just a political solution but a cultural and spiritual one—a way to revive the West's lost soul and restore its place in the world.

The Tragic Vision of Yockey

Francis Parker Yockey's philosophy is tragic—a vision of history as a cycle of rise and fall, of civilizations born in the fire of creativity only to be consumed by their own success. It is a vision that sees decline not as an anomaly but as the natural outcome of greatness, a process driven by the very spirit that once gave the civilization life.

Yockey's ideas are deeply pessimistic, rooted in a belief that the West is in its twilight, its *Cultural Vitalism* spent, its spirit exhausted. His critique of materialism, rationalism, liberalism, and democracy is a lament for a lost world—a world where culture and spirit were once the driving forces of civilization, now replaced by the hollow pursuit of wealth and power.

Yet, Yockey's vision is also one of hope—a hope that the West can revive its lost *Cultural Vitalism* and resist the forces of decline. His vision of *Imperium* is a call to return to the higher values that once defined Western civilization, a plea for a unified Europe to stand against the tide of decay and restore its place in the world.

In the end, Yockey's philosophy is a reflection of the tragic nature of history itself—a story of rise and fall, of civilizations born in the fire of creativity only to be consumed by their own success. It is a vision that sees decline not as an anomaly but as the natural outcome of greatness, a process driven by the very spirit that once gave the civilization life.

Yockey's lament for the West is a mournful cry for a civilization that has lost its way—a civilization that once stood at the pinnacle of human achievement, now facing the twilight of its existence. Yet, in that twilight, Yockey sees the possibility of renewal—a chance for the West to revive its lost soul, to restore its *Cultural Vitalism*, and to reclaim its place in the world.

[58]

American Samuari

[59]

AMERICAN SAMURAI Vol:1 Davey Crockett and American Mythos

Davy Crockett is most likely more myth than reality, but who cares? Crockett is an American myth worth telling. Solider, politician, hunter, and outdoorsmen par excellence, dies in a hail of gunfire at the Alamo, portrayed by John Wayne. I don't give a damn if it is all fluff, give me that mythos over having to hear about Ruby Bridges and Nelson Mandela any day.

Crockett is everything you ever thought was cool about America, hell he was what the gunfighters in the Wild West thought was cool. He was born to a poor family where his grandparents were murdered by Creek and Cherokee Indians, and his uncle was held captive for seventeen years by said Indians. His father sold him into indentured servitude twice. He fought the Creek Indians under Andrew Jackson, came home fathered six kids, became a senator, quit, and went out in a blaze of glory at the Alamo.

The details don't matter. What does matter is what he represents. He was the physical embodiment of what American men idolized in the 19th century. He is the spirit that exists in us all to tame the wild, the Faustian desire to conquer infinite space (to channel Spangler). Going into the frontier and becoming a master of the unknown.

Four legends from the *Ballad of Davy Crockett* are important here.

-He killed a bear when he was three
-Fought the Creek Indians single-handedly
-Went to Washington to "drain the swamp"
-Died in a blaze of glory at the Alamo

Each of these myths listed above represents an important expression of the American Frontiersmen as an incarnation of the American Spirt.

First, three-year-old Davy Crockett, still in the 18th-century equivalent of pampers didn't kill a bear. However, this legend provides us with the understanding that Davy is born on the frontier. He is not a man from Europe coming to chase adventure, he is adventure. Davy is the American with no memory of Europe, born here and molded by the experience alien to their grandfathers. Killing the bear shows the mastering of the frontier and the taming of the wild. Just like Davy Americans will have to do this from a young age because the frontier gives no quarter even to children. So, Davy is born in America, thrown into the untamed wilderness, and conquers the beast.

Fighting the Creek Indians single-handedly. Davey Crockett had a small and insignificant role in the war against the Creek Indians. What this legend represents is relatively self-explanatory. If you're on the frontier you're going to have to fight Indians at some point, therefore, you might as well fight as Davey did. You may find yourself alone in new territory when off in the distance a group of hostile Indians appears on the horizon. There is nowhere to run and if you do you will only die tired. So, you think back to Davy and how he single-handedly bested some Creek Indians, and you muster up the courage to do the same. Results may vary but fighting Indians was part of the job, and Davy Crockett taught you that. Again, it's a myth but it serves a greater purpose of transmitting the dangers of the frontier and how to face them.

Mr. Crockett goes to Washington; it didn't turn out like the Frank Capra film and Crockett probably didn't go to "drain the swamp". In fact, he did the typical political dance and made deals and mostly squabbled over land rights. The purpose of this element of the Davey Crockett story is to exhibit the desire of Americans to clear out the crooked politicians and have it done by a "good ole boy". Just like Mr. Smith in the aforementioned Frank Capra film he doesn't really do much and is pretty disillusioned with the whole process. Crockett did go to Washington and here the legend tells Americans that when the government is being, the government you might just have to go and fix it yourself, just wear a coonskin cap not a red one, and when that doesn't work well, you can always go to Texas.

Last and most importantly we have the last stand at the Alamo. Savagely disillusioned with politics (the Whigs had hoped to run him for President), Crockett said "Since you have chosen to elect a man with a timber toe to succeed me, you may all go to hell, and I will go to Texas." At the Alamo Davy Crockett and less than two hundred men fought to the death against Santa Anna and two thousand of his troops. The actual events are shady, and it probably didn't go down like John Wayne said it did. The result was the same Texas gained independence (if only for a little bit) and Santa Anna ran away in drag. The imagery is important two hundred brave Texans fighting to the last man in hand-to-hand combat to slow the Mexican Army. Every decent nation needs a last stand, the Greeks have Thermopylae, the Brits have Rorke's Drift, the Scots have Bannockburn, etc. Americans found theirs at the Alamo. Crockett dying in a blaze of glory in many ways symbolize the death of the frontier. Just as Davy Crockett's mythological life represented the life of the young American nation so his death was a precursor to the fall of the frontiersman and the rise of the cowboy right in the heart of Texas.

Davy Crockett was the prototypical frontiersman, the perfect representative for a newly formed nation ready to expand. His myth carries the elements that help build the nation. The traits of heritage Americans that founded and built America. When people ask "What is American culture?" remember that buried deep beneath the rainbow flags and the fast-food restaurants, lies men like Crockett waiting to be repurposed for a new generation of Americans.

[60]

American Samurai Vol:2 Sgt. York and the hero's journey

Alvin York was just a simple farmer and blacksmith from the hills of Tennessee. From this simple beginning, Alvin would be thrust into the pantheon of American mythological heroes by WWI. His journey would take him from the backwoods of Tennessee to the fields of France and back. Alvin's story is not a myth, yet the journey was mythological so mythological in fact we might call it the archetypal hero adventure. Before we go making grandiose claims, we should refamiliarize ourselves with the quintessential expert on the heroic and comparative mythology Mr. Joseph Campbell.

Joseph Campbell's *Hero with a Thousand Faces* was published in 1949 it is a work of comparative mythology in which Campbell compares the mythological journeys of archetypal heroes across cultures. Campbell's book summarized these stories into a monomyth that he dubs the "hero's adventure". For Campbell, the hero's adventure has seventeen steps.

The Call to Adventure
Refusal of the Call
Supernatural Aid
The Crossing of the First Threshold
Belly of the Whale
The Road of Trials
The Meeting with the Goddess
Woman as the Temptress
Atonement with the Father
Apotheosis
The Ultimate Boon
Refusal of the Return
The Magic Flight
Rescue from Without
The Crossing of the Return Threshold
Master of the Two Worlds
Freedom to Live

I know that's a lot of criteria to meet for Alvin York but luckily Campbell gives our hero an out. The hero does not have to meet all seventeen steps or even complete them in order. In Alvin's case, we are going to look at nine steps following three acts (I. Departure, II. Initiation, III. Return).

The Call to Adventure
Refusal of the Call
Supernatural Aid

The Crossing of the First Threshold
Belly of the Whale
The Road of Trials
The Ultimate Boon
The Crossing of the Return Threshold
Freedom to Live

Act I: Supernatural aid/ Call to adventure/ Refusal of the call.

Our hero comes from humble beginnings. Alvin was born in a small cabin in Tennessee. The third of eleven children, he grew poor with a farmer and part-time blacksmith for a father. His father died when he was young and Alvin took up the mantle of provider, and by all accounts, he was good at keeping his family fed and clothed. Alvin had another side. He was a violent drunk. His drunken brawls even left his best friend dead, and he spent time in and out of jail. But where would our story be without a little redemption?

Supernatural Aid:

Alvin was struck by lightning his road to Damascus moment had come. Alvin ran straight to the church repented of his sins and was a changed man. Well, that's how it happened in the film *Sergeant York.* In real life, Alvin's mother and wife spent years witnessing to him until he eventually saw the light and dedicated his life to Christ. He repudiated his life of violence and chose pacifism and a life of quiet farming.

God has a funny habit of having different plans for us than we have for ourselves. While Alvin wanted to lay low and farm, life sent him a draft notice, he was going to France.

Call to adventure/Refusal of the call:

Alvin's call to adventure was World War One, this poor farm boy from Tennessee was being sent to France to fight and kill Germans. That was a problem because Alvin had just promised he was going to stop doing both of those things. Uncle Sam had different plans, so Alvin sought conscientious objector status on religious grounds which he was granted. See back in WWI if you were a conscientious objector, you still had to serve in the Army and Alvin was a man of his word and refused to seek discharge from the Army.

So, Alvin unwilling to fight but willing to serve Alvin was sent to France.

Act II: Crossing the first threshold/Belly of the Whale/Road of trials

Alvin entered the belly of the whale or as it is commonly called Company G, 328th Infantry, 82nd Division of the U.S. Army. In France, Alvin began to speak with his company commander, Captain Edward Courtney Bullock Danforth Jr., and his battalion commander, Major G. Edward Buxton. The result of these conversations was a change of heart. Alvin came to the conclusion that he could in fact fight and so was sent to the front lines of the Argonne.

We pause here to take a moment to remind those of just how bad The Meuse-Argonne offensive was. It was the largest front-line commitment of troops by the U.S. Army in World War I, and also its deadliest. Between September 26 – November 11, 1918, some 1.2 million French and American troops did battle with 450,00 Germans. The result was an Allied victory but at the cost of 122,063 dead or wounded Americans, 70,000 French casualties, and 126,000 German casualties. This is the belly of the whale where Alvin would face his road of trials.

Belly of the Whale / Road of Trials.

October 8, 1918, Alvin and his unit were tasked with taking a German machine gun nest near hill 223. The German machine guns had stopped the Americans dead in their tracks. Alvin would later recall.

Our boys just went down like the long grass before the mowing machine at home. Our attack just faded out ... And there we were, lying down, about halfway across [the valley] and those German machine guns and big shells getting us hard

Corporal York, four NCOs, and thirteen Privates were ordered to infiltrate the German lines to take out the machine guns. York and his men managed to infiltrate behind enemy lines and overran a group of Germans preparing to attack U.S. troops. While handling the prisoner, a German Machine gun opened up on them. In an instant six Americans were dead and three wounded. York described the events later.

And those machine guns were spitting fire and cutting down the undergrowth all around me something awful. And the Germans were yelling orders. You never heard such a racket in all of your life. I didn't have time to dodge behind a tree or dive into the brush ... As soon as the machine guns opened fire on me, I began to exchange shots with them. There were over thirty of them in continuous action, and all I could do was touch the Germans off just as fast as I could. I was sharp shooting ... All the time I kept yelling at them to come down. I didn't want to kill any more than I had to. But it was they or I. And I was giving them the best I had.

York fought his way to the machine gun at times relying on his side arm to do the job. York managed to reach the machine gun and began to pick the Germans off one by one. Eventually, Imperial German Army First Lieutenant Paul Jürgen Vollmer, emptied his pistol trying to put an end to York. Failing to so much as wound York, and realizing his mounting losses, he offered in English to surrender to York

York and seven men then marched 132 Germans back to American lines. Upon his return, Brigadier General Julian Robert Lindsey remarked: "Well York, I hear you have captured the whole German army. " Famously York replied: "No sir. I got only 132."

Act III: Crossing the Return Threshold/ Freedom to Live/ Ultimate Boon

Alvin returned home in the spring of 1919 and soon after found himself in the national spotlight. His story was circulated around the country as the marketability of a soft-spoken simple man from the country was realized. Alvin refused offers to profit from his new fame and instead retired to a simple life of farming.

Freedom to Live.

Alvin formed the Alvin C. York Foundation which was geared toward increasing educational opportunities for children in rural Tennessee. Alvin did speaking tours to raise money for his foundation. Audiences were left wanting as York chose not to speak about his time in the Argonne. York when asked to speak out about the war said

"I occupied one space in a fifty-mile front. I saw so little it hardly seems worthwhile discussing it. I'm trying to forget the war in the interest of the mountain boys and girls that I grew up among."

The York Foundation would not survive the Great Depression and he would spend the rest of his life working in various government jobs. He would campaign for U.S. involvement in WWII and try to enlist when the war came through at fifty-four he was too old. Alvin and his wife Gracie had ten children over the course of their marriage. Alvin would go on to live a relatively quiet life until his death on September 2, 1964.

Ultimate Boon.

Indestructible life or limitless bounty is what Campbell calls Ultimate Boon. For Alvin York, this comes in the form of the myth that surrounds him. He would be the subject of the highest-grossing film of 1941 starring Gary Cooper as York (a role that would win Cooper the Oscar). For York, his heroic feats in the Argonne Forrest live on, they live long past his life on earth. Earning him a place in the pantheon of the U.S. Armies stored history.

Alvin's Monomyth

Joseph Campbell's monomyth that condensed the epic tales from across time and culture was lived by Alvin York. While his life followed a universal heroic path complete with redemption and divine intervention. His story is uniquely American. Alvin York was shaped by the distinctive conditions of the Appalachian hills. The grit and determination cultivated from a life of subsistence farming kept Alvin going. The spiritual confidence fashioned from the evangelical tradition rendered the fear of death as nothing more than a whisper. The masterful use of M1903 to dilute German resistance to the equivalent of a turkey shoot. These are all traits crafted by the American experience making Alvin's hero's journey extraordinarily American.

As Campbell and others have shown the hero's journey has a formulaic nature. The long and arduous path from a self-effacing mortal man to a heroic demigod is marked by a set of challenges where the would-be hero faces adversity and loss, is cast into the belly of a whale, baptized by the fires of combat, touches the divine and returns home born again.

Alvin York lived the hero's journey. His life was

as real as yours and mine. Yet he walked the path of the mythological heroes of old. Alvin heeded the call to adventure that drew him from the hills of Tennessee. Crossing the threshold into a war-torn France. Enduring the road of trials where he faced death in the Argonne Forest. Finally returning home and discovering the freedom to live a normal life and raise a family. In the end, the ultimate boon, his memory lives on forever in the halls of the heroic, worthy in its own way of standing next to the likes of Odysseus or Beowulf. For every young boy whose imagination turns sticks to rifles, there the mythological spirit of Sargent York lives.

[61]

American Samurai Vol:3 Braveheart Edition

No William Wallace is not American, no, *Braveheart*[68] is not remotely historically accurate. I don't care and neither should you. Here at the Slaughterhouse, I make the rules, and William Wallace, or more accurately Mel Gibson's portrayal of him in *Braveheart* has been given honorary American Samurai status. Besides being one of the best films ever made and the peak of Mel's acting and directing, there is something uniquely American about *Braveheart*. Despite the fact that it takes place in the Scottish Highlands hundreds of years before America is founded, it has that rugged individualism that defines the most American of figures, the cowboy.

In many ways, William Wallace is a cowboy because he embodies the archetypal heroic nature of a cowboy. It could be the overlap of the values of the Scottish highlander and the American cowboy, or the residue of Scottish culture being felt in America. It seems ridiculous, William Wallace the cowboy, if I am going to make claims like that, I should explain how I see the American cowboy in terms of myth and archetypes before I start mixing metaphors.

The cowboy is to Americans, what the samurai is to the Japanese, the knight is to the English, or the highlander is to Scotland. He is the archetypal hero, a mythological creation formed by the culmination of their shared values, projected in a form uniquely crafted from the self-image of each culture. For America, the archetypal hero takes the form of the cowboy.

It is important to understand the distinction between forms and their representation in reality. If you have not familiarized yourself with the platonic idea of forms, now would be a good time to do so. If not, I will provide a quick explanation.

In your mind, you have the idea or form of a cowboy, if you close your eyes, you can picture him. The cowboy of your mind is abstract, he is all cowboys and no particular cowboy. In reality, the cowboy can vary in size, and hair color, he can be from Colorado or Texas, but he is the representation of the form of a cowboy in reality. You know a cowboy when you see one because he represents the form of a cowboy. in addition, there is also the abstract quality of the form so a person or thing can have a cowboy-ness without being a cowboy.

If that didn't make sense, I'm sorry. I'm not a philosophy teacher and you didn't come here for armchair philosophy. You are welcome to turn back anytime.

If you are still here, we have the form of a cowboy, which is the basis of our archetypal American hero. The archetypical part is, in essence, all those qualities that would be ideal for a cowboy all rolled into one individual. They may even take physical form; I would argue that the chivalric code or the bushido code (to keep with our knight and samurai example) are these ideal heroic characteristics (or archetypes) written down or even legalized. For Americans, this may be John Wayne's or Clint Eastwood's portrayals of a cowboy. The code their characters lived by (in most films) embodied the unwritten code of the cowboy.

So, each culture has its unique archetypal heroic form. The heroic form is the aggregate of all heroic qualities most valued by a given culture and crafted in their self-image. The stories that a culture tells to communicate that form and how it acts out the heroic values become the myths that define them. These myths at their core tell us how ideally that form navigates the world.

The archetypal heroic myth of the cowboy is (more often than not), a man who has gone west in the wake of the Civil War looking to start over. He puts his violent past to bed and begins with the help of a woman, to enjoy a quiet life. He is thrust into conflict after the loss of a loved one at the hands of a tyrannical authority. He is joined by others who have been terrorized by the same tyrannical authority and is reluctantly thrown into the role of hero. Once he accepts this role nothing short of dying will stop him from seeing justice and order restored.

Okay, now, how do William Wallace and *Braveheart* fit in here? Well, if you read the above paragraph, you now know the basic synopsis of *Braveheart*. I am not going to give you a rundown of the plot points. If you have seen it, you already know, if you haven't then stop and go watch it now. If you have seen the film then you will recognize William Wallace's story in, many Western classics such as *High Plains Drifter*, *Hang'Em High*, *The Shootist,* etc.

The cowboy is the archetypal hero of founding stock America, his stories are the myths bringing to life the conflict between the ideal hero and a flawed world. When we hear stories or watch movies about cowboys, we are watching our ideal heroic form, we are seeing ourselves as we want to be seen and as we want the world to view us. The cowboy is all that is good in our culture fighting to stay good in a wicked world.

Watching *Braveheart,* it is easy to see the cowboy-ness in its themes, Wallace is self-reliant, honest, brave, and loyal, he is a reluctant hero and a good friend. He values freedom and peace. When forced to fight he sees it to the end. He is a cowboy, an American samurai, or maybe the Scottish immigrants brought their archetypal hero with them and that spirit lives in us, maybe the Cowboy is an American Highlander?

[62]

American Samurai Vol:4 The Teleology of Conan

I recently watched *Conan the Barbarian*[69] the 1982 action/fantasy film starring the third most famous Austrian Arnold Schwarzenegger. On the surface, *Conan* seems to be a twelve-year-old boy's dream full of women, war, and weapons, however, under the pulp dime novel façade there is depth. One of the most famous lines from the film gives us a peek into the philosophical motivations of Conan. There is a scene in which Conan is asked "What is best in life?" he responds "To crush your enemies, to see them driven before you, and to hear the lamentations of their women". This question is in effect "What is the purpose of life?". For Conan, the answer is total victory over his enemies. It's not victory for victory's sake, it's what victory contains, which is honor and glory, that drive Conan they are his telos.

Let's talk about telos.

Telos. That's a word you won't hear used, often, at least not today. Ever since, modern education saw fit to remove philosophy from its curriculum teleology, ontology, epistemology, and metaphysics, in general, have become little more than foreign sounds to Western ears. This as far as I can tell is because we live in a post-enlightenment world that sees everything through a reductionist materialist lens, and in a world that is purely material there is no place for philosophy and the metaphysical, but I digress.

Back to telos...

Telos in the most basic terms means end goal or purpose. Generally speaking, there are four causes or four explanations to the question "why?"', in Aristotelian thought: the material, the formal, the efficient, and the final. Don't worry about the other three, for now, we are only concerned with the final cause or Telos. The final cause of anything is its end goal or telos. So when philosophers use the term teleological or teleology it is simply to explain something by looking at the result. For example, the telos of sex is procreation, that is to say, the purpose or goal of sex is reproduction, and everything else is window dressing, or in philosophical terms functions.

Telos can encompass all of life, and there are telos that are subordinate to other telos. A subordinate telos simply serves as the means to achieve a higher telos. The telos of a blacksmith is the production of swords, while the soldier uses the sword o kill his enemies. In turn, the telos of the blacksmith and soldier serve a higher telos to a king, his telos being to maintain the kingdom. So, the telos of the blacksmith and soldiers are directed at the higher telos of the king.

So, everything has a telos, including you and me, and we have subordinate telos that serve higher telos. This creates a hierarchical teleological structure oriented towards an ultimate purpose. This begs the question of what telos is the highest order? Answering this would be to understand how to properly orient your life toward the ultimate good. All in all, you would be able to say what the meaning of life is. Don't get your hopes up I am not answering that and neither are you but let's consider what much smarter people have to say on the subject.

Aristotle would say that the telos of life is eudaimonia. Eudaimonia roughly translates to happiness, not in a material sense, this is more purpose-driven. For Aristotle happiness is reasoning well or acting rationally according to virtue this is his telos, true happiness. Again, this is not momentary happiness, it is necessary for man to rationally act according to virtue, for his entire life because one day does not make a man happy. The active component cannot be understated, for Aristotle, it is not enough to be virtuous you must actualize that virtue, and you will have a good life, you will find eudaimonia.

What if there is more? Something bigger than you or your society, or your Instagram account?

St. Thomas Aquinas would build on Aristotle's ideas. Aquinas understood that all humans are ordered toward God, and humans are defined by their intellect. These two components God and intellect are central for St. Thomas Aquinas, he explains man's telos this way.

"Since all creatures are ordered to God as to an ultimate end, all achieve this end to the extent that they participate somewhat in His likeness. Intellectual creatures attain it in a special way, that is, through their proper operation of understanding Him. Hence, this must be the end of the intellectual creature, namely, to understand God."

Aquinas's understanding of the telos of man is helpful. He points us to the simple fact, that to know God is the ultimate telos. It's the top of the hierarchy, that all other telos are subordinate to. If all this holds, then everything oriented properly will point to God as the ultimate telos.

Where does that leave us? Our modern culture does not recognize greater meaning much less God. There is no hierarchy in modernity and egalitarianism rules the day. If all things are equal then nothing can take priority, and to understand the ultimate telos of life you have to point to that which is prior to all things, that which all telos orient themselves to, God. If knowing God is the ultimate telos then we would expect people or nations that orient themselves in that way to achieve great things since all telos then are oriented toward the highest goal resulting in the full actualization of their potential.

To be fair we may not all agree that the telos of man is to understand God, however, it should be understood that a ship needs a crew, a crew needs a captain, and that captain needs a compass. Without this, a ship will wander the high seas aimlessly. As far as I can tell America, and the West have no captain and the people playing captain have Jack Sparrow's compass to guide them (if you don't know it points to what the wearer of the compass wants not north). That's just something to think about, I digress (again).

Back to Conan, honor, and glory may seem a shallow answer in comparison to God as the ultimate telos, but it's still more profound than what our current culture offers. Conan at least looks outside of himself to find his purpose which comes from a sense of honor (as honorable as a barbarian can be). It is something to strive toward and drives him to do great things. Those who follow Conan will orient themselves toward him and share in his glory. It's all temporal Conan's telos is not higher-order reasoning but it's better than what we are currently sold.

Nietzsche famously quipped "God is dead", this was not a celebration but a warning. He knew that when the West embraced enlightenment ideals and rejected God that absurd rationality would remove God as the ultimate telos. This would leave a vacuum and if it was not filled man would atrophy and his spirit would die. Nietzsche spent his life trying to fill that vacuum with the Übermensch. It didn't work; it turns out man cannot be his own compass. The last century and the beginning of this one have borne this out. Decades and generation after generation with no telos have led us here.

Fyodor Dostoyevsky saw this coming. In *Notes from the Underground* written in 1864, he describes what happens to men without telos.

"Shower upon him every earthly blessing, drown him in a sea of happiness, so that nothing but bubbles of bliss can be seen on the surface; give him economic prosperity, such that he should have nothing else to do but sleep, eat cakes and busy himself with the continuation of his species, and even then out of sheer ingratitude, sheer spite, man would play you some nasty trick"

Sounds familiar? Well, if Russian literature isn't your thing, consider what Christ said in Mark 8:36

"For what will it profit a man if he gains the whole world, and loses his own soul?

You see Conan orders himself to something greater, he is orientated to a telos greater than himself. Conan has a telos that guides him. Aquinas, Aristotle, and the truly great men in history have all had telos. Why should we be any different? You may not be ready to have God as your telos, but consider how much better your life would be if you simply oriented yourself to something greater than a phone screen.

I know you read all that and probably wondered how is this tied to America. Well, I'll keep this part short. Look at America or the West, in general, today, do they seem to have a telos? Does it not simply seek progress for progress' sake? When America had a telos it settled the west, built the Panama Canal, and went to the moon. We got really far in the 20th century because our conflict with the Soviet Union gave us a telos but they are no more. With no great enemy and endless material prosperity, America has become directionless, simply spinning her wheels in search of a purpose.

I won't end on such a down note. Consider the Reconquista for seven hundred years the Moors ruled Spain, and the Christian armies isolated to a small three-hundred-mile area in the north of Spain and driven by their love of God and country managed to drive the Moors out and place the King and the Church back in power. That is the power of telos.

[63]

American Samurai Special Edition: Once more into the Breach

They don't make them like they used to that line runs through my head often, especially when I look at our current leaders. I can't help but laugh, (albeit due to gallows humor) when I see our current President, or the last one, or the one before him, and before him, that list starts to get quite long before you began to run into men that one might call a leader much less heroic. Most are not even that remarkable, I would make exceptions for Nixon, Eisenhower, and Teddy Roosevelt. Nixon because he was a true outsider and might be the highest IQ president we have had. Eisenhower because he was a general that happened to become president, not a politician, but rather a logistical genius, and a hero of WWII. Lastly, there is

Teddy Roosevelt, he was a renaissance man, cowboy, soldier, boxer, and adventurer a remarkable man all around. Only one of these I would call heroic.

But first, we should consider what it is to be a heroic man. A heroic man is quite different than a hero. Audy Murphy is a hero, Alexander the Great is a heroic man, Firefighters on 9/11 are heroes, but Napoleon is a heroic man. There is a difference between a hero and the heroic, a hero is defined by a moment in time, the heroic man defines his time during the moments he is alive. For me, when it comes to the heroic I always turn to Thomas Carlyle. In a collection of Carlyle's lectures titled *On Heroes and Hero Worship*[71] Carlyle describes heroic men in this way,

"They were the leaders of men, these great ones; the modelers, patterns, and in a wide sense creators, of whatsoever the general mass of men contrived to do or to attain; all things that we see standing accomplished in the world are properly the outer material result, the practical realization and embodiment, of Thoughts that dwelt in the Great Men, sent into the world: the soul of the whole world's history, it may justly be considered, were the history of these."

For a better understanding of the heroic in Carlylean terms, you must read *On Heros and Hero Worship*. It is a masterful work and a great introduction to Carlyle, who if you don't know is a master of the English language and one of the most prolific writers of the 19th century. But for now, consider how he describes the heroic man, does any world leader in living memory fit that description? I doubt our current age has produced such a man, in terms of US Presidents only one of the three Nixon, Eisenhower, and Teddy Roosevelt can be considered heroic in Carlylean terms.

The answer is obviously, Teddy Roosevelt. He truly was a man of heroic substance. A man of will, who never settled, lived a life of adventure, and left his mark on the world. Teddy is America, in the same way, Frederick the Great is Prussia or Alfred the Great is England. Those men are the great leaders of their nations who embody the greatest attributes that their people manifest. If you had one former president to represent America is there even a question? Maybe Washington, but I would argue that America as an idea was not formed fully and so he could not represent its full potential. Teddy is it, he is America, say what you will about his politics, but Teddy was American exceptionalism in carnate.

There is a clear deletion between the presidents' pre and post-Teddy Roosevelt. Of the first twenty-six Presidents, nineteen had military service, out of these, seventeen saw combat and led men on the battlefield. These were men of action leaders shaping a new nation. Post-Teddy, we have ten Presidents who were in the military, but they saw little if any combat and were not men of marital status but were simply in the military due to WWII. They did not have to scrap and fight they inherited an established country; they were handed the keys to the castle so to speak. These men were mostly politicians or intellectuals first, not great leaders, and not heroic.

The post-heroic age is how I would describe the era following Teddy's time in office. From Woodrow Willson onward it is clear (to borrow terms from Machiavelli) that the "Lions" have given way to the "Foxes", or in layman's terms, we could say the general gives way to the politician. This transformation has resulted in dimensioning returns, with each subsequent president being less qualified to lead than the last. It would be laughable to compare the credentials of Biden, Obama, Trump, Clinton, or Bush to any President in the 19th century. Do you really think Obama is the same caliber man as Washington or Jackson? You may not like their politics but those are leaders of men, and Obama is...Obama. This is why I consider this time post-heroic these men who lead us now are forgettable, weak, and uninspiring, they stand on the shoulders of giants and say they are flying.

To highlight my point I am going to give a quick overview of Teddy Roosevelt the last President of the heroic age. While you read, I ask that you keep in mind the Presidents we have had in our lifetime and compare them to those of the past. Not in terms of policy but as a man, as a leader, and as a representative of America.

Teddy Roosevelt was the 26th president of the

United States, and the youngest man to hold that office. Born into a well-to-do family in New York, he was a sickly child suffering from severe asthma. He would overcome this weakness through strenuous exercise and will. He took up rowing, boxing, and wrestling as ways to overcome his weakness. This focus on strength would define Teddy for the rest of his life.

He was home schooled and later went to Harvard. There he studied biology and became a published ornithologist. He also went on to be runner-up in an intramural boxing tournament, a member of the literary society, a member of the Porcelain Club, was editor of *The Harvard Advocate* and graduated magna cum laude. After graduation, he went on to write *A Naval History of the War of 1812.* Already he has a more impressive resume than most but Teddy was more than an intellectual and he would prove that.

Teddy grew up with a romantic notion of the West and dreamed of being a cowboy. Eager to prove himself a man and more than the child of New York aristocrats he built a ranch in the Dakota Territory using the inheritance from his father's estate. His time as a rancher led him to create the Boone and Crockett Club with the goal of the conservation of large game animals and would foreshadow his creation of the National Parks Service. Ranching proved hard and Teddy was determined to live the life of a cowboy always on the ground working his cattle, but after the particularly harsh winter of

1886-1887, his cattle were wiped out. With his dreams of ranching gone, he returned to New York.

Now he was no longer just a New York Intellectual, he was a cowboy, a man of the people, he had experienced the West and returned home a new man. Teddy decided to get into politics, first in the Civil Service Commission, then as the New York City Police Commissioner. As Police Commissioner he regularly walked the officer's beats late at night despite the danger, again proving his willingness to get his hands dirty.

Continuing to climb the ladder, he was then appointed Assistant Secretary of the Navy by William McKinley. This would not last long because during this time tensions built to war with Spain. The United States blamed the sinking of the USS Maine in Cuba on the Spanish. "To hell with Spain, remember the Maine", became a rallying cry for pro-war politicians and Roosevelt was one of its loudest proponents.

Yet ever a man of honor, he put his money where his mouth was. While most politicians were eager to send young men to fight and die for the safety of their offices in Washington, Teddy was not. Despite protests from his wife and friends he resigned from his post in Washington eager to join the fight.

This was a different time it was an age of adventure, so Teddy didn't join the Army instead he raised a volunteer regiment. Made up of Ivy Leaguers, professional and amateur athletes, upscale gentlemen, cowboys, frontiersmen, Native

Americans, hunters, miners, prospectors, former soldiers, and tradesmen, and under the command of former Confederate general Joseph Wheeler. They truly embodied their namesake the "Rough Riders". After training for six weeks in San Antonio, they went to Florida, commandeered (one might argue illegally) a naval ship, and headed to Spain to fight.

The defining moment for Teddy was the charge up Kettle Hill at the battle of San Juan Heights. Under his leadership, the Rough Riders became famous for their suicidal assault on July 1, 1898. While in support of the regular army, Roosevelt and the Rough Riders charged Spanish rifles head-on. Roosevelt on his horse (aptly named Texas) rode back and forth between rifle pits at the forefront of the advance up Kettle Hill, an advance that he urged despite the absence of any orders from superiors. Teddy recalled the events,

"I sent messenger after messenger to try to find General Sumner or General Wood and get permission to advance, and was just about making up my mind that in the absence of orders I had better 'march toward the guns,' when Lieutenant Colonel Dorst came riding up through the storm of bullets with the welcome command 'to move forward and support the regulars in the assault on the hills in front.' "

Eventually, with his horse tangled in barbed wire, and his rifle empty Teddy led the charge on foot with only his revolver in hand. The Rough Riders took the hill and later when asked to recall the battle Teddy simply called it "the greatest day of my life". The victory came at a cost of 200 killed and 1,000 wounded. For his actions on the day, Teddy was awarded The Metal of Honor.

After the war, he would be Governor of New York, and Vice President under William McKinley. After Mckinley was assassinated Teddy would become US president. I will stop here, this is not a full biography and I believe I have already laid the groundwork for my larger point so the details can be spared.

Now compare that life with, Biden, Trump, Obama, etc. politics aside can you truly say they are even worthy of being in the same room? You cannot honestly say yes, and any attempt to do so would be disingenuous at best and herein lies my point, we are in the post-heroic age. Leaders willing to fight and die like Teddy are almost foreign to us. We are so starved for heroes we latch on to anyone with a glimmer of potential. That desire for the heroic man does not go away. C.S. Lewis said in *Present Concerns*

"Where men are forbidden to honor a king they honor millionaires, athletes, or film stars instead: even famous prostitutes or gangsters. For spiritual nature, like bodily nature, will be served; deny it food and it will gobble poison."

It may be that we are just living through the "good times create weak men phase of our civilization" True hardship is alien to our leaders they are the products of lavish decadent lifestyles. It matters not what side of the political spectrum you sit it is easy to see that we are not ruled by our betters. Alexander famously rode out in front of the Macedonian cavalry, Teddy rode in front on Kettle Hill. One can almost imagine Teddy giving Shakespeare's "Once More Into the Breach" monologue from *Henry V* to his men. Our current leaders would probably struggle to even fully understand the willingness of a king to fight with his men, much less rally them to battle and charge into the breach.

Where does that leave us? There does not appear to be a heroic man on the horizon, and even if there were the current regime is still too powerful to allow him to come to power. The post-heroic age may be the winter of our civilization, but after winter comes spring; the time to grow our own heroes, to inspire the heroic in our sons, to give them that which the world denied us, to give them the tools to truly be great.

The cultivation of character falls on us. We have to instill heroic values in our children. You must choose what kind of man you want to raise a heroic man or a modern man, but you must decide because if you don't the world will decide for you.

[64]

American Samurai Vol:6 War Machine

Larry Allen Thorne was a man who lived a life of adventure that took him from the icy hills of Finland, the Russian step, the Gulf of Mexico, and finally to the jungles of Vietnam. A special forces pioneer, he escaped prisons and POW a camp and hitchhiked across the United States. A man who hated communists so much that he fought them under any military that gave him the chance. He was a man of determination who faced the world head-on and earned his place in American lore. In short Larry Allen Thorne was a warrior par excellence. He is without a doubt an American Samurai.

Larry Allen Thorne was born Lauri Allan Torni on May 28, 1919 in Viipuri Finland. He was a typical Finnish boy who excelled at sports and school. He entered business school in his late teens but that is where normal life ended for Lauri. Like so many men of his generation war would come to define his life and in November of 1939, the Soviet Union invaded Finland signaling the beginning of the Winter War.

Lauri joined the Finnish military with Jaeger Battalion 4. His unit fought in multiple battles at Lake Ladoga, eventually taking part in encircling and destroying the Soviet battalions at Lemetti. The Moscow peace treaty brought the 105-day war to a close in March of 1940; Lauri's performance on the battlefield didn't go unnoticed and by the war's end, he was commissioned as a 2nd lieutenant and shipped off to officer training school.

Lauri remained in the reserves and was sent for a seven-week training exercise in Vienna, Austria with the Waffen-SS. He returned to Finland fifteen months later and was soon back at war. The Second Russo-Finnish War (Continuation war) was a joint German-Finnish offensive launched against the Soviet Union in June of 1941. The conflict was part of WWII and was aimed at pushing back the Soviets and reclaiming territory the Finns lost in the Winter war.

During the Second Russo-Finnish war he was recognized by the Germans as an Untersturmfuher (Junior storm leader). He was given command of a unit informally known as Detachment Torni (named after himself). His unit penetrated deep into enemy territory and gained a reputation for their ruthless and efficient performance on the battlefield. During the battle of Ilomasti Lauri's detachment inflicted such high casualties on the Soviets that a bounty of 3,000,000 Finnish marks was placed on his head. For his actions, Lauri was given the Mannerheim Cross the Finnish equivalent of the Medal of Honor, but in September of 1944 the Finnish government signed a peace treaty with the Soviets and demobilized their military but Lauri still had a bone to pick with the Soviets.

The Finnish military may quit but Lauri had grown to hate communists and was looking for any chance to oppose them. He joined a pro-German resistance movement aimed at combatting the Soviet presence in Finland and left for saboteur training in Germany with the goal of organizing resistance against the Soviets; Lauri's training was cut short and with no way of returning to Finland he joined a German unit and returned to the front lines of the Eastern Front of WWII. He would continue to fight for the Germans until he was captured by British troops and imprisoned in a POW camp.

Lauri escaped the POW camp in 1945 and returned to Finland. He was promptly arrested by Valpo (Finnish State Police) but just like the POW camp, Lauri escaped. His freedom didn't last long as he was arrested a second time, this time he was tried for treason due to his joining the German military. He was sent to Turku Prison and escaped again only to be recaptured and placed back in prison. So if you are keeping count he has now escaped one POW camp, a jail, and a prison. He would not have to escape a fourth time instead he received a pardon and was released.

I am going to pause here. You may find it hard to understand how an SS officer is an American hero or at best worthy of being admired and that is forgivable; public school education lacks any form of nuance and to truly understand history you're gonna need a heavy dose of nuance.

You need to understand the threat that communism was to Europe, it is not an exaggeration to call it biblical. The Communist armies of the Soviet Union were on the march committing atrocities from Ukraine to Mongolia. At the same time, communist revolutionaries had/were causing civil wars in Spain and Portugal and had come close to overthrowing the governments in Italy, France, and Germany. So it is no surprise that for many any chance to fight the communist was welcomed. The SS offered this chance. Men from France, Sweden, Norway, North Africa, the Middle East, and even Russia joined the ranks of the SS to fight communism. So keep that in mind when evaluating Mr. Thorne, he just hated communists.

Now back to the story.

Lauri eventually left for Sweden to stay with Baroness von Essen who help harbor fugitive Finnish soldiers following the war. Lauri may have been pardoned but he was still guilty of treason in the court of public opinion. He found worked as a carpenter for a time before he decided to head to the Americas. He traveled undercover as a Swedish seaman aboard the SS Bolivia headed to Caracas, Venezuela. He spent time with other exiled Fins and decided America would offer him a better opportunity so he hitched a ride on a Swedish cargo ship and while in the Gulf of Mexico, he jumped ship and swam into Mobile Bay. From Mobile, he hitchhiked to New York City.

In June of 1950, the Lodge-Philibin Act allowed for the recruitment of foreign nationals into the American military. Much like Operation Paperclip which saw the recruitment of top Nazi scientists brought to America (most famously Warner von Braun) The Lodge-Philin Act made sure the American Military could also utilize the skills of their former enemies and Lauri was the perfect candidate for this program.

Lauri entered the US Army in 1954 and adopted the name, Larry Allen Thorne. Years of fighting in Finland, Russia, and Germany had left Larry with an invaluable skill set and it wasn't long before the Army recognized this. He joined the special forces and was sent to OCS and commissioned a first lieutenant. Larry would see two tours of duty in Vietnam where he received two Purple Hearts and a Bronze Star for valor. Larry Allen Thorne died on October 18, 1965, after his helicopter crashed during a mission. He was posthumously awarded the Legion of Merit, and the Distinguished Flying Cross, and was promoted to the rank of major. His remains were not discovered until 1999 but not fully identified until 2003 after which his body was buried in Arlington National Cemetery.

Larry Allen Thorne is the embodiment of a warrior. His life was changed forever by the invasion of the Soviet Union into Finland from that moment on war became his art. Few men can boast a resume of martial experience in the modern age like Larry Allen Thorne. He was a true warrior, a man born to fight, a man who faced down the Red Army, his own government, and the Vietcong. In the end, he died doing what he loved and for men like Larry Allen Thorne, there is no other option. He lived and died as a true American Samurai.

[65]

American Samurai: Crimson Courage

When we think of Alabama's military history, we most often think of The Creek Indian War and the Civil War, we think of names like Andrew Jackson and William C. Oates we think of Horseshoe Bend and Gettysburg. What doesn't come to mind is WW1, yet the First World War produced one of the greatest battles in Alabama's history.

> *In time of war, send me all the Alabamians you can get, but in time of peace, for Lord's sake, send them to somebody else.*
> *– General Edward H. Plummer*

At the heart of this story is the 4th Alabama Infantry Regiment, a unit often regarded as the descendant of a Confederate unit with the same name and number. Interestingly, there had not been a 4th Alabama between the end of the Civil War in 1865 and its reestablishment by the Alabama legislature in 1911 as part of the militia. The newly activated 4th Alabama Infantry Regiment, led by Major William Preston Screws, a seasoned regular army officer, assembled at Vandiver Park in Montgomery, Alabama, in late June of 1916 and was sent to the border to hunt Pancho Villa.

The journey of the 4th Alabama did not stop at the Mexican border; it continued to expand and evolve. The regiment underwent basic infantry training at Vandiver Park from July 4, 1916, to October 22, 1916. Later, Major Screws led about 1,300 officers and men to Nogales, Arizona, for advanced infantry training, which lasted until March

As World War I engulfed the globe, Alabama rallied to support the Allied forces. Among the many battalions that stood tall during the Great War, the 167th Infantry Regiment, known as the "Alabamians," stood out for its unwavering determination and indomitable spirit. Under the leadership of Colonel C. A. Scruggs, this regiment proved its mettle during the Battle of Croix Rouge Farm.

The Battle of Croix Rouge Farm fought on the blood-soaked soil of France, witnessed a fierce clash between the 167th Infantry Regiment and the formidable 4th Prussian Guards of Germany. It was a battle of attrition, where bravery and tenacity were the only currency. On that fateful day of July 26, 1918, the 167th Infantry Regiment faced intense enemy fire as they pushed forward with unwavering resolve.

The Alabamians encountered a daunting landscape: muddy trenches, shell-pocked fields, and camouflaged machine guns. Yet, they moved forward undeterred, answering the call of duty with a resolute "Hell with the bayonet." The 1st Battalion, under Major John W. Carroll, and the 3rd Battalion, led by Major Dallas B. Smith, valiantly charged through thin woods towards their objective – the Croix Rouge Farmhouse.

The attack was relentless, and the casualties were heavy. Men fell to enemy fire as they fought valiantly, exhibiting remarkable leadership by example. Major Carroll's 1st Battalion faced staggering losses, with 65% of its troops either killed or wounded in the initial assault. Captain Lacey Edmundson's D Company saw 80% of its men killed or wounded during the fierce battle.

Amidst the carnage and chaos, Lieutenant Robert Espy, a true hero of the Croix Rouge Farm, led a successful second effort. With men from various companies coming together in a united front, they displayed unwavering courage and determination, pushing the Germans back and seizing the farmhouse.

However, the 3rd Battalion, under Major Dallas B. Smith, faced its share of trials. Despite being pushed back and reorganizing into two small companies, a ray of hope emerged as First Lieutenant Edward R. "Shorty" Wrenn and his detail brought a one-pounder mortar. Wrenn's efforts turned the tide of the battle, saving the day and earning him the Distinguished Service Cross and the French Croix de Guerre.

As night fell on July 26, the battlefield was shrouded in darkness and drizzling rain. The Alabamians showed unwavering determination, attending to the wounded, while burial parties somberly laid the fallen soldiers to rest. It was a night of sorrow and heartache, yet the Alabama spirit endured.

The Battle of Croix Rouge Farm was a testament to the courage, resilience, and unbreakable spirit of the Alabamians. Their sacrifice and heroism stood out amidst the chaos of war, exemplifying the true meaning of valor. While the battle itself was overshadowed by the larger conflict of World War I, it remains a crucial chapter in Alabama's history – a chapter that deserves remembrance and recognition

In the annals of Alabama's military history, the Battle of Croix Rouge Farm finds its place alongside the gallant actions of William Oates and other celebrated military heroes. These brave Alabamians, with their bayonets held high, exemplified the spirit of their state, displaying unwavering determination and courage in the face of adversity. As we remember the valor of those who fought at Croix Rouge Farm, let us honor their sacrifice and ensure that their memory lives on, undiminished and forever etched in the fabric of Alabama's rich military heritage.

[66]

American Samurai: Crusader Addition,"The Great Escape"

On December 25, 1100, in the city of Jerusalem, Baldwin I was crowned King of Bethlehem. Following the death of Godfrey of Bouillon, a power struggle between Bohemond I of Antioch and the supporters of the late Godfrey of Bouillon landed Baldwin in the position of King. The early years of his reign were dedicated to consolidating power over Palestine, a fact not lost on his Muslim neighbors, particularly the Shi'ite Fatimids of Egypt and their vizier al-Afdal, seeking revenge for their previous humiliation by the First Crusader.

In May of 1101, Baldwin received news that Al-Afdal had amassed a large army advancing on the Holy City under the command of Sa'ad al-Daulah. In response, Baldwin headed south and chose to hold his ground at Ramla, awaiting the Fatimid's next move. For the next three tense months, a standoff ensued. As summer waned, the Egyptians, seizing their last opportunity to take Ramla, began advancing on the city.

Growing impatient, Baldwin decided to confront the Egyptians head-on, a risky endeavor given the vast numerical superiority of the opposing forces. Despite summoning troops from across the kingdom and knighting every eligible squire, he faced the daunting challenge with just 260 knights and 900 footmen. Christian estimates of Muslim manpower at the time varied widely, but it was evident that the Christians were heavily outnumbered, with some estimates nearing 200,000 Muslim troops.

At dawn, Muslim forces appeared on the horizon, prompting King Baldwin to kneel before the True Cross, confess his sins, receive mass, and address his troops:

"Come then, soldiers of Christ, be of good cheer and fear nothing, fight, I beseech you, for the salvation of your souls... If you should be slain here, you will surely be among the blessed. Already the gate of the kingdom of Heaven is open to you. If you survive as victors, you will shine in glory among the Christians. If, however, you wish to flee, remember that France is indeed a long distance away."

The ensuing battle was chaotic. The Christian vanguard was quickly decimated, and the entire army found itself encircled. Baldwin, leading a reserve force, charged into the fray, and under the force of his attack, rank after rank of Fatimid troops buckled. In the retreat that followed, Sa'ad al-Daulah was killed, leaving around 5,000 Muslim soldiers dead alongside 80 Christian knights and an unknown number of infantry.

Baldwin rested easy, knowing the Muslim forces had been repelled. However, in May of 1101, he learned of Muslim troops near Ramla once again. Baldwin, along with 200 knights, rode out to meet what he believed was a small Muslim force, only to encounter a formidable army of 20,000 men.

With no escape, Baldwin chose to fight, charging head-on into the Egyptian army. Although surrounded, Baldwin's courageous charge turned the tide, and most of the knights were cut down. A handful of survivors, including Baldwin, managed a fighting retreat and found refuge in a fortified tower at Ramla.

The situation took a dire turn that night as Baldwin faced the prospect of certain death in the morning. In a difficult decision, he chose to escape, and under cover of night and in disguise, Baldwin and five of his fiercest knights fled the encircled tower. Their escape was not without challenges, they were soon spotted by Muslim patrols and a Frankish knight named Robert took the lead, charging with sword in hand, mowing down the enemy. He was soon cut down along with two more of Baldwin's knights.

The remaining knights continued the fight and Baldwin mounted a horse and made a dash toward

Jaffa with the Muslim troops in pursuit. As the sun began to rise he hid in an overgrown thicket to avoid detection but the Muslim troops wasting no time set it ablaze. Baldwin was badly burned but managed to escape once again.

Baldwin spent the next two days without food or water, wandering the desert to avoid Muslim patrols. Eventually, he headed north to Arsuf, where he found some safety. Contacting Hugh of Flachenburg, who had arrived with 80 knights at Arsuf upon hearing of the Muslim assault, Baldwin commandeered an English pirate ship and sailed south with Hugh and his knights riding along the coastline.

Arriving at Jaffa, they found the city under siege from land and sea. With a bold decision, Baldwin flew his royal banner, signaling to the people that their king was alive. Despite Muslim ships closing in, Baldwin narrowly made it to port.

Upon returning to the city, Baldwin found a grim situation. The city had nearly surrendered, believing him dead after the Muslim commander Sharaf al-Ma'ali presented the body of Gerbod of Windeke, (who bore a strong resemblance to the king). Sharaf had Gerbod's arms and legs cut off, wrapped his body in royal purple, and paraded it around the city, encouraging surrender. Even the Queen believed Baldwin dead and began planning to abandon the city. It was at this critical moment that Baldwin's colors were seen flying from the harbor.

Baldwin's return rallied his troops, shaking the Muslim army, which began to retreat. While Baldwin saved Jaffa, his loyal knights at Ramla's tower were not as fortunate. The morning after his escape, Muslim forces set fire to the tower. Opting to die in battle rather than burn, the knights made a last stand. The only survivor, Conrad of Germany, fought with such intensity that it is said "he stood encircled by the dead and dying," prompting the Muslim troops to offer to take him alive.

[67]

American Samurai Vol:8 Blood and Plunder

"This burning ship was a beautiful spectacle, the scene being wild and picturesque beyond description. The black clouds were mustering their forces in fearful array. Already the entire heavens had been overcast. The thunder began to roll, and crash, and the lightning to leap from cloud to cloud in a thousand eccentric lines. The sea was in a tumult of rage; the winds howled, and floods of rain descended. Amid this turmoil of the elements, the Dunbar, all in flames, and with disordered gear and unfurled canvas, lay rolling and tossing upon the sea. Now an ignited sail would fly away from a yard, and scud off before the gale ; and now the yard itself, released from the control of its braces, would swing about wildly, as in the madness of despair, and then drop into the sea. Finally the masts went by the board, and then the hull rocked to and fro for a while, until it was filled with water, and the fire nearly quenched, when it settled

to the bottom of the great deep, a victim to the passions of man, and the fury of the elements."

-Raphael Semmes

Raphael Semmes stands out as one of the greatest naval officers in American history. A professor of philosophy and English literature, he served as the inspiration for Captain Nemo in Jules Verne's "Twenty Thousand Leagues Under the Sea." Known by his sailors as "Old Bee's Wax", and by his enemies as the "American Nelson," Semmes is most famous for his command of the CSS Alabama. Under his leadership from 1862 to 1864, the *Alabama* captured or sank more than 60 Union ships, making it one of the most successful commerce raiders in naval history.

Raphael Semmes was born in Charles County, Maryland, on September 27, 1809, the fourth child of Richard and Catherine Middleton Semmes. He was orphaned at an early age and raised by an uncle with whom he shared the same name. Semmes secured an appointment as a midshipman in the U.S. Navy in 1826. Over the next four years, Semmes served on the sloop of war Erie and the frigate Brandywine as they showed the flag in the Caribbean, along the coast of South America, and in the Mediterranean. During extensive periods of leave and in spare moments aboard ship, he studied law. In 1832, at 22, Semmes was commissioned a passed midshipman, but three years slipped by before he trod the deck of a ship as an officer. During those years, he opened a law practice and gained admission to the Maryland bar.

in 1835, Semmes served as acting master of the frigate *Constellation*, tasked to support the Army during the 1835–42 Second Seminole War. Semmes took command of the small steamer *Lt. Izard* in 1836, operating on the Withlacoochee River in what ultimately became the state of Florida. In 1837 he married Anne Elizabeth Spencer He relocated his family to Alabama, settling in Mobile. Though establishing a new life ashore, Semmes also served on or commanded several naval vessels engaged in hydrographic surveys, gaining knowledge that would one day enable him to truly prosper as a captain.

From 1846 to 1848, Semmes participated, afloat and ashore, in the Mexican-American War. In October 1846, he received command of the *Somers*. While serving on blockade duty near Verde Island, the vessel encountered a squall, capsized, and sank within 10 minutes with heavy loss of life. Exonerated by a court of inquiry, Semmes marched with the Army to Mexico City. His journals formed the basis for a popular 1851 memoir, *Service Afloat and Ashore During the Mexican War*.

At the outbreak of the Civil War Semmes was offered command of the merchant steamer *Habana* by Confederate Secretary of the Navy Stephen Mallory. The *Habana* was built in 1859 and condemned by the naval service as unsuitable for use as a warship. Despite the subpar vessel, Semmes was eager and accepted, leaving immediately for New Orleans.

After two months the *Habana* was repurposed and commissioned the CSS *Sumter*. While the *Habana* was being transformed into the *Sumter,* the first Confederate privateers were put to sea as President Abraham Lincoln ordered a blockade of the Southern coast. The blockade proved incapable of stopping Semmes and on June 31st he outmaneuvered the sloop of war USS *Brooklyn* and broke into the open sea. Three days later, Semmes and crew claimed their first victim, *Golden Rocket*.

17 prizes followed (seven burned, 10 sent into friendly ports under bond) the *Golden Rocket*. Despite the success of the ship Semmes never loved his cruiser. At slightly over 470 tons, the 184-foot bark-rigged steamer was slow, under steam and sail. Its armament included just four 32-pounder smoothbores, an 8-inch shell gun, and, for a short while, a relatively ineffective howitzer on a land carriage, to put it plainly weapons that while acceptable for terrorizing merchants were far from suitable for engaging even the smallest of Union warships.

Nevertheless, *Sumter's* six-month pillaging voyage through the Caribbean and across the Atlantic to Spain would not have been possible under anyone but Semmes. His remarkable knowledge of the ocean, coastlines, weather, and shipping lanes, along with exquisite navigational skills, allowed him to find his targets and survive the crucible of the sea and naval combat. During his time on the *Sumter*, Semmes' belief in harsh discipline gained him a reputation as a dictator, but his leadership skills melded officers and seamen composed of disparate nationalities into an effective crew.

At the end of 1861, a sea-battered *Sumter* crossed the Atlantic to Cadiz, Spain. They proved a force of nature, having nearly closed Union merchant traffic in the Caribbean, propelling neutral shippers to withhold goods from Union ships, and diverting Union warships from the blockade and amphibious support to hunt them. More importantly, Semmes and the *Sumter* allowed the international community to reconsider neutrality (as a student and practitioner of maritime law, Semmes was careful to avoid trampling the neutrality of other nations). Though Spain evicted the *Sumter*, British Gibraltar welcomed her.

During their expedition, the *Sumter* had been badly damaged and without extensive repairs, she could neither sail nor evade waiting Union blockaders, so Semmes paid off his crew and laid up the vessel. Having not found a ship to replace her Semmes and his first officer, Lieutenant John McIntosh Kell, left Gibraltar expecting to return home, but fate would give them eternal fame, and for Semmes, fame home held the same name: Alabama.

John Laird Sons and Company launched *Enrica*—a

screw sloop of war designed specifically for commerce raiding for the Confederate Navy—on July 29, 1862, at Birkenhead, England. Just before the Union had the chance to confiscate her hull Confederate agent James Dunwoody Bulloch gathered a mostly British civilian crew and sailed for Terceira Island in the neutral Azores, where Semmes joined Bulloch and was promoted to captain. While in the Azores the *Enrica* was reconditioned with material delivered by Agrippina.

Semmes, in constant fear of the arrival of a Union warship, forced his officers and men to complete the outfitting as fast as possible. Four days later, Semmes moved the ship into international waters and dropped anchor. The captain and his 23 officers stood on the deck proudly wearing their new Confederate grey and formally commissioned the Confederacy's most powerful seagoing warship, the CSS *Alabama*. Only one condition remained: Semmes needed a crew, and that required persuading the British sailors aboard to join the Confederate States Navy. When a passionate speech about honor and duty failed, Semmes decided to appeal to the sailors in a language all their own. Semmes offered the crew signing bonuses, double wages, and prize money (to be paid in gold). Money talked and eighty-three men signed on and with a full crew, Semmes turned the *Alabama* westward to begin a voyage that would influence naval doctrine for the next five decades.

The *Alabama* exemplified the best in naval construction of commerce raiders for its time. Displacing 1,050 tons and 220 feet in length, the vessel had bark-rigged sails and a 300-horsepower steam engine (the propeller could be detached and lifted from the water to reduce drag when under sail). Capable of achieving 10 knots under steam or sails (13 knots when conditions allow the use of both). The *Alabama* could outrun any Union warships let alone the merchant ships it preyed upon. And if speed failed the *Alabama* could put up a fight, Semmes' raider sported: six 32-pounder smoothbores (three per side), a long-range 100-pounder Blakely rifle on a forward pivot mount, and an 8-inch smoothbore shell gun on an aft pivot. A condenser provided fresh water, and hold space allowed for three months' worth of provisions. With no homeport open to him, Semmes' major concerns were coal (he could carry no more than 10 days' worth), provisions, and fresh crew members. Like the pirates that came before him Semmes knew the answer to his circumstances was obvious: Let the enemy provide.

Semmes asked and he received, on Sept. 4, 1862, the *Alabama* entered whaling grounds off the Azores, and the *Alabama* approached the Massachusetts whaler *Ocmulgee* under cover of a British flag (Semmes would use various neutral flags over the next two years). When the whaler responded by raising the Stars and Stripes, the colors of Dixie quickly replaced the false ensign, and a warning shot brought the enemy to a halt. A boarding party took control of the vessel and began stripping it of anything useful, while Semmes encouraged its crew to sign on with the *Alabama*.

For the next couple of months, Semmes and crew would utilize the same modus operandi to great success. Occasionally, prisoners crowded the deck of the *Alabama* until Semmes could land them in neutral territory or transfer them to a ship communed as a prisoner cartel (usually because it held large neutral cargoes, and Semmes knew the dangers of offending neutral powers). Occasionally, a prize crew sailed the captured ship to a neutral harbor, unloaded the prisoners, and returned to neutral waters to burn the vessel. Semmes never missed an opportunity to capitalize on his enemy's mistakes, by using their vessels against them. On at least one occasion Semmes retained a ship as a temporary collier (cargo ships fitted to carry coal) when the *Agrippina* failed to make its rendezvous. Semmes even transformed one prize into a raider, CSS *Tuscaloosa*, which captured two prizes of its own before it was plundered by the British.

Burning ships and sunken hulls followed Semmes' wake from the shores of Canada, through his former cruising grounds in the Caribbean and the Gulf of Mexico. It was in the Gulf where Semmes attempted to disrupt the Union invasion of Galveston, Texas. On Jan. 11, 1863 Semmes engaged and destroyed the converted passenger steamer USS Hatteras. Semmes rescued the surviving Yankees and fled to the Caribbean before turning south for Brazil in hopes of evading the Union.

Semmes continued to take prizes as he sailed from the coast of Brazil toward Cape Town, South Africa. Arriving in August 1863, the crew of Alabama enjoyed a brief reprieve from heavy weather and Union warships. It is while docked in South Africa that the *Alabama* inspired the song "Daar kom die Alibama" ("There comes the Alibama") a traditional Afrikaans and Cape jazz song.

With his crew rested and his ship repaired, Semmes crossed the Indian Ocean to the China Sea, raided in the Strait of Malacca, and returned to Cape Town via India and the east coast of Africa. Far from home in foreign waters, Semmes found the occasional prize and had to elude the pursuing USS *Wyoming*. In late March 1864, the *Alabama* returned to Cape Town, with an exhausted crew and weary captain.

Semmes had spent most of his time since 1861 at sea, and the constant stress of command had taken its toll. With the knowledge that his family had returned to the South, Semmes worried about how to get money to Elizabeth to support her and the children. By 1864 it was clear that without intervention by neutral France or Great Britain, The Confederacy would not survive. The *Alabama* was not doing much better— with coppering warped and dangling, she was slowed and her wooden bottom was open to the ravages of worms; her boilers were rusted and her old munitions were, damp, and rusted by the salty air. To make things worse, the Union press had labeled Semmes and his crew as pirates, a disgraceful charge he could not combat while at sea. There was nothing else Semmes could do, so he decided to make for a neutral European port, where he could weigh three options refurbish, lay-up, or sell *Alabama*.

On June 11, 1864, a legendary voyage ended as the *Alabama* dropped anchor in the harbor of Cherbourg, France.

In 22 months, the *Alabama* burned 54 Union merchant ships, bonded 10 others, and defeated a Union warship in open battle. He had driven the Union's surviving merchant marines to the shelter of foreign flags as he redirected Union combatants from blockade duty. In so doing, Semmes had provided hope for the survival of the Confederacy.

The story of Semmes and Alabama could have ended there, but on June 14 the screw sloop of war USS Kearsarge, under Captain John Winslow, entered Cherbourg Harbor after hearing rumors of the raider's presence and took up a blockading station three miles off the harbor. Semmes never one to back down saw a chance to secure a victory that might shift the European powers from neutrality. Semmes rallied his crew and set out on the *Alabama* to meet the enemy as French civilians gathered to watch.

Seven miles offshore, canons thundered as the

warships pounded each other at 1,000 yards or less. *Alabama's* gunners fired rapidly and wildly. The *Kearsarge*, partly protected by iron chains that hung amidship, fired more deliberately. Semmes proved more capable but the failure of many of the *Alabama's* corroded shells to explode sealed her fate. An hour into the battle, the raider, its sides pierced and decks awash with blood, began to settle by the stern. With his steering damaged and boilers flooded, Semmes chose to save what remained of his crew and raised a white flag. Wounded in the arm, the Rebel captain tossed his sword into the sea and then leaped in after it and watched as the *Alabama* slipped beneath the waves, ending its short but courageous career as a commerce raider.

> *No one who is not a seaman can realize the blow which falls upon the heart of a commander, upon the sinking of his ship. It is not merely the loss of a battle — it is the overwhelming of his household, as it were, in a great catastrophe. – Raphael Semmes*

Rescued by a British yacht, Semmes and 40-odd crewmen escaped the enemy. They returned by blockade-runner to the Confederacy where Semmes was promoted to admiral and given command of the James River Squadron, in support of the Army of Northern Virginia until the abandonment of Richmond forced their destruction in April 1865. Commissioned a brigadier general (the only officer to hold flag rank in both navy and army), Semmes led his sailors to join General Joseph E. Johnston's army in central North Carolina. They arrived too late for battle, but in time to be paroled with the remainder of the army at Durham Station.

The war over he returned to his wife Elizabeth and their children but could not escape Yankee animosity. He was arrested in December 1865 on a charge of treason and spent four months in prison before Congress found insufficient cause to hold him. After his release, Semmes taught Philosophy and English literature at Louisiana State Seminary, wrote his memoirs, and practiced law in Mobile. On August 30, 1877, Admiral Raphael H. Semmes, one of the best-known and most beloved Southern heroes, and greatest naval commanders of any age departed this world on his final voyage., but his memory and the memory of the *Alabama* lives on in the sounds of sailors as they sing *Roll Alabama Roll...*

When the Alabama's keel was laid
Roll, Alabama, Roll
Twas laid in the yard of Jonathan Laird
O Roll, Alabama, Roll
Twas laid in the yard of Jonathan Laird
Roll, Alabama, Roll
Twas laid in the town of Birkenhead
O Roll, Alabama, Roll

Notes

The Lonely Future

1) "Crossing the Uncanny Valley of Voice." Sesame, https://www.sesame.com/research/crossing_the_uncanny_valley_of_voice

Paradise Lost and Found: TFR, Liberation, and the World to Come.

2) Lee, Seung-Joo, and Jennifer K. Lee. "South Korea's Extraordinary Fertility Decline." RAND Corporation, 5 July 2022, https://www.rand.org/pubs/commentary/2022/07/south-koreas-extraordinary-fertility-decline.html.

3) Romanian Justice Ministry. DECRET Nr. 770 din 1 octombrie 1966. Retrieved 11 July 2022.

4) Legal Library of the Soviet Union. Decree of the Presidium of the Supreme Soviet of the Soviet Union of July 8, 1944 (in Russian). 8 July 1944. Retrieved 25 February 2012.

5) Legal Library of the Soviet Union. Decree of the Presidium of the Supreme Soviet of the Soviet Union

of July 8, 1944 (in Russian). 8 July 1944. Retrieved 25 February 2012.

6) Our World in Data. “Children per Woman (UN).” Our World in Data, https://ourworldindata.org/grapher/children-per-woman-un

7) Waldman, Barry M. “Trends in the Labor Force Participation of Women.” Monthly Labor Review, vol. 125, no. 5, May 2002, U.S. Bureau of Labor Statistics, https://www.bls.gov/opub/mlr/2002/05/art2full.pdf.

8) American Institute for Behavioral Research and Technology. “Male College Enrollment and Completion.” AIBR, https://aibm.org/research/male-college-enrollment-and-completion/#:~=Men%20are%20also%20less%20likely,to%2043%25%20for%20male%20students.

9) DataPandas. “Fertility Rate by Country.” DataPandas, https://www.datapandas.org/ranking/fertility-rate-by-country

10) Milton, John. Paradise Lost. Edited by Alastair Fowler, Longman, 1998. Book 1, lines 102-103

The Scent of Postmodernism

11) Scent of a Woman. Directed by Martin Brest, performances by Al Pacino, Chris O’Donnell, and James Rebhorn, Universal Pictures, 1992.

12) It’s a Wonderful Life. Directed by Frank Capra, performances by James Stewart, Donna Reed, and Lionel Barrymore, RKO Radio Pictures, 1946.

13) Catholic Church. Catechism of the Catholic Church. 2nd ed., Vatican Press, 1997, p. 565.

14) Baudrillard, Jean. Simulacra and Simulation. Translated by Sheila Faria Glaser, University of Michigan Press, 1994.

15) Lyotard, Jean-François. The Postmodern Condition: A Report on Knowledge. Translated by Geoff Bennington and Brian Massumi, University of Minnesota Press, 1984.

16) Jencks, Charles. The Language of Post-Modern Architecture. 3rd ed., Rizzoli, 1984.

17) John Paul II. Veritatis Splendor. Vatican Press, 1993.

Circling The Drain with Cthulhu

18) Data Republican. Data Republican, https://www.datarepublican.com/

Anonymity and Alienation: The Cultural Impact of Non-Places

19) Augé, Marc. Non-Place: Introduction to an Anthropology of Supermodernity. Translated by John Howe, Verso, 1995.

You're called to be meek. That doesn't mean what you think it does.

20) Etymonline. (n.d.). Meek. Online Etymology Dictionary. Retrieved 6/28/2024, from https://www.etymonline.com/word/meek

21) Etymonline. (n.d.). Gentle. Online Etymology Dictionary. Retrieved 6/28/2024, from https://www.etymonline.com/word/gentle#etymonline_v_6011

22) Xenophon. Xenophon in Seven Volumes, 7. E. C. Marchant, G. W. Bowersock, tr. Constitution of

the Athenians. Harvard University Press, Cambridge, MA; William Heinemann, Ltd., London. 1925.

23) St. Ambrose, quoted in St. Thomas Aquinas' Catena Aurea, as translated by St. John Henry Newman.

24) Aquinas, Thomas. Summa Theologica. Edited by Thomas Gilby, OP. 60 vols. Cambridge: Blackfriars, 1966. (ST II-II q.1, a.1.)

The Forgotten Tradition of Christian Combat

25) Nicolaus von Jeroschin. The Chronicle of Prussia. Translated by Mary Fischer. Farnham: Ashgate Publishing, 2010.

26) Ibid

27) Ibid

28) Frowe, Helen. "Just War Theory." Internet Encyclopedia of Philosophy. University of Tennessee at Martin. Accessed September 15, 2024. https://iep.utm.edu/justwar/.

29) Bernard of Clairvaux. In Praise of the New Knighthood. Translated by Conrad Greenia, ocso. In Bernard of Clairvaux: Treatises Three, Cistercian Fathers Series, No.19. Kalamazoo, MI: Cistercian Publications, 1977, 127-145

30) Ibid

31) Ibid

32) Ibid

33) Charles G. Addison, The History of the Knights Templars, the Temple Church, and the Temple. London: Longman, Brown, Green, and Longmans, 1842.

34) Regula Pauperum Commilitonum Christi et Templi Salomonis (The Rule of the Poor Fellow-Soldiers of Christ and of the Temple of Solomon), by Bernard of Clairvaux (1090-1153), in In Praise of the New Knighthood (Liber ad milites Templi: De laude novae militae).

35) The Rule of the Teutonic Knights (Ordo domus Sanctae Mariae Teutonicorum). Translated by Uwe Ziegler. In The Military Orders: History and Heritage, edited by Malcolm Barber. Aldershot: Ashgate Publishing, 1994.

36) Regula Pauperum Commilitonum Christi et Templi Salomonis (The Rule of the Poor Fellow-Soldiers of Christ and of the Temple of Solomon), by Bernard of Clairvaux (1090-1153), in In Praise of the New Knighthood (Liber ad milites Templi: De laude novae militae).

37) Acta Hospitalis: A Compendium of Records from the Administration of the Hospitaller Knights, Including Reports from the Grand Master.

38)Ibid

39) The Rule of the Teutonic Knights (Ordo domus Sanctae Mariae Teutonicorum). Translated by Uwe Ziegler. In The Military Orders: History and Heritage, edited by Malcolm Barber. Aldershot: Ashgate Publishing, 1994.

40) I translated this from Middle German, and it may not be accurate as I could not find a direct translation in any historical records.

The Twilight of Warriors

41) Evola, Julius. Meditations on the Peaks: Mountain Climbing as Metaphor for the Spiritual Quest. Translated by Guido Stucco, Inner Traditions, 1995.

42) Evola, J. (1992). Meditations on the Peaks: Mountain Climbing as Metaphor for the Spiritual Quest. Inner Traditions.

43) Janetta Rebold Benton, Materials, methods, and masterpieces of medieval art, p. 257 (Greenwood Publishing Group, 2009)

44) Michael Smathers (January 27, 2022). "Bushido: The Samurai Code of Honor

45) Jünger, Ernst. The Glass Bees. Translated by Allison L. Strassheim, Seaver Books, 1989.

46) Grossman, D. (1995). On Killing: The Psychological Cost of Learning to Kill in War and Society. Little, Brown and Company

American Foederati

47) Defense One. "Military Services Upping Recruiting Goals After Rebound in 2024." Defense One, 10 Oct. 2024, https://www.defenseone.com/policy/2024/10/military-services-upping-recruiting-goals-after-rebound-2024/400698/.

48) Machiavelli, Niccolò. The Art of War. Translated by Christopher Lynch, University of Chicago Press, 2003,

The Cosmocentric Family and the Fate of Empires

49) Hubbard, John. The Fate of Empires

50) Miller, Stephen. "Lex Julia de Adulteriis (18 B.C.)." California State University, Northridge, https://www.csun.edu/~hcfll004/Adulteriis.html.

51) Baker, C. S. (Charles S.). “Augustus and Marriage Legislation.” California State University, Northridge, https://www.csun.edu/~hcfll004/AugMarriage.html

52) Tacitus, Publius Cornelius. The Annals of Imperial Rome. Translated by Michael Grant, Penguin Books, 1956, Book 3, Chapter 25.

53) Tacitus, Publius Cornelius. The Annals of Imperial Rome. Translated by Michael Grant, Penguin Books, 1956, Book 3, Chapter 25.

54) Gibbon, Edward. The Decline and Fall of the Roman Empire. Edited by David Womersley, Penguin Classics, 1994, vol. 1From Common Origins:The Cultural Fabric of America

55) Jay, John. The Federalist Papers. Edited by Clinton Rossiter, Penguin Books, 1961, pp. 34-40.

56) Jay, John. The Federalist Papers. Edited by Clinton Rossiter, Penguin Books, 1961, p. 35.

Catabolic Opportunity

57) Greer, John Michael. How Civilizations Fall: A Theory of Catabolic Collapse. New Society Publishers, 2008.

Perception and the Art of Reality: A Woman Simply is, but a Man Must Become

58) Axios Coaching, Substack, https://axioscoaching.substack.com/.

59) McKay, Brett, and Kate McKay. The Art of Manliness. www.artofmanliness.com. Accessed

The Technological Tide Instinct: Intellect, and Dasein

60) Spengler, Oswald, et al. The Decline of the West. United Kingdom, Oxford University Press, 1991

61) Ellul, Jacques. The technological society. United States, Knopf, 1964.

62) Heidegger, Martin. The Question Concerning Technology, and Other Essays. United States, Garland Pub., 1977.

63) Heidegger, Martin, and Macquarrie, John. Being and Time. United Kingdom, HarperCollins, 2008.

Dixie Noir: The Rebirth of Southern Gothic

64) "Dixie Noir: The Making of a Genre." Virginia Gentry Magazine, https://www.virginiagentrymagazine.com/p/dixie-noir-the-making-of-a-genre.

From Dystopia to Divine: Christian Symbolism in Gene Wolfe's Book of the New Sun

65) Wolfe, Gene. The Shadow of the Torturer. Tor Books, 1980.

Wolfe, Gene. The Claw of the Conciliator. Tor Books, 1981.

Wolfe, Gene. The Sword of the Lictor. Tor Books, 1982.

Wolfe, Gene. The Citadel of the Autarch. Tor Books, 1983.

The Secret of TeenagerdomSlopification vs Infantilization

66) Fiddler's Greene, Substack, https://substack.com/@fiddlersgreene

67) Deceneus. Deceneus, Substack, https://substack.com/@deceneus.

American Samurai Vol:3 Braveheart Edition

68) Braveheart. Directed by Mel Gibson, performances by Mel Gibson, Sophie Marceau, and Patrick McGoohan, Paramount Pictures, 1995.

American Samurai Vol:4 The Teleology of Conan

69) Conan the Barbarian. Directed by John Milius, performances by Arnold Schwarzenegger, James Earl Jones, and Sandahl Bergman, Universal Pictures, 1982.

American Samurai Special Edition: Once more into the Breach

70) Carlyle, Thomas. On Heroes, Hero-Worship, and the Heroic in History

About the Author

John Slaughter is a veteran of the United States Marine Corps, a husband, father,r and German Shepherd appreciator. He lives in Alabama with his wife and two sons.

Also by John Slaughter

In the heart of the South, where vice and virtue collide, J.D. Hooks is a disillusioned private eye navigating a world steeped in corruption. Haunted by the ghosts of war and the shadow of his father's death, Hooks finds himself in Arcadia, Alabama—a place where justice bends to the will of the powerful and sin runs rampant.

When Evelyn Sinclair, an enigmatic heiress, walks into his office with a missing persons case and a cryptic plea for discretion, Hooks is thrust into a deadly game of lies, betrayal, and violence. As he digs deeper, secrets emerge—ones that threaten to destroy not only the Sinclair family's reputation but also his fragile grasp on morality.

With a city ruled by a ruthless crime syndicate and a femme fatale who straddles the line between lover and adversary, Hooks must untangle a web of deception that extends far beyond a missing girl. But in a world where the law is written in blood, can he find redemption, or will his quest for truth be his undoing?

Crimson Veil

"John Slaughter has synthesized the heat, decay, and ghosts of the Southern Gothic genre with the violent, urban undertow of noir. It is rare to find a dramatization of the subtle, crushing weight of a man at war with himself searching for stakes that galvanize him to victory that remain not only grounded in reality but genuinely compelling. Slaughter accomplished this in Crimson Veil, and he's made it possible for the reader to long for circumstances that are lost to history and bleakly dangerous. Many have said history is over, and it was fair to make a similar assumption about fiction. But history, like fiction, is still marching on through the muck of modernity only through feats of strength to usher in more enriching times. Crimson Veil is one of those feats."

— Arthur Mena, Blood and Rain Podcast.

Made in the USA
Columbia, SC
07 April 2025

fee4b672-589b-47db-a644-345c831fc88cR01